THE 20-MINUTE
author

THE 20-MINUTE
author

STEP-BY-STEP WORKBOOK

MAJA WOLNIK

First published in 2021 by Maja Wolnik.
Copyright © 2021 Maja Wolnik
2ND EITION. All rights reserved.

This book or any portion thereof may not be reproduced or used in any manner whatsoever without the express written permission of the author except for the use of brief quotations in articles or reviews.

ISBN PRINT: 978-0-6450416-4-4
ISBN EBOOK: 978-0-6450416-5-1

Editing Services by Caitlin Freeman of Get Bookified
Portrait Photography of Maja Wolnik by Clare Stephens

Book Cover, Typestting and Layout Design Copyright © 2021 Maja Creative
Art Direction by Maja Wolnik of Maja Creative
Graphic Design by Monika Brzeczek of Maja Creative
www.majacreative.com

dedication

This book is dedicated to you, dear reader, for daring to
shine brightly. May your voice be heard. May your story be told.
May your wisdom be shared. May your book make an impact
in the life of one and many.

With love and light,
Maja xx

table of contents

INTRODUCTION 12
1: THE 20-MINUTE AUTHOR 14
2: MINDSET HACKS TO BANISH IMPOSTOR SYNDROME .. 30
3: START WITH YOUR WHY 48
4: DEVELOP YOUR IDEAL READER PROFILE 60
5: JOIN THE 20-MINUTE AUTHOR 20-DAY CHALLENGE 78
6: GET YOUR BOOK CHAPTERS SORTED 88
7: HOW TO SELECT A BEST-SELLING BOOK TITLE 100
8: SECURE YOUR UNIQUE BOOK TITLE 112
9: MOTIVATION CHECK-IN 122
10: START PROMOTING YOUR BOOK NOW 132
11: BOOK COVERS THAT CONVERT 150
12: PROVE YOUR AUTHOR CREDIBILITY 164
13: PAGE TURNING DESIGN 176
14: YOUR BOOK QUESTIONS ANSWERED 192
15: BOOK EDITING FUNDAMENTALS 200
16: HOW TO GET OUT OF A BOOK RUT 212
17: AUTHOR BRANDING..224
18: REVERSE ENGINEER YOUR BOOK 240
19: CASE STUDY—THIS BOOK 252
20: YOU ARE AN AUTHOR 262
21: YOUR BOOK MAPPING SESSION 274
MORE WAYS THAT WE CAN HELP YOU 286
ABOUT THE AUTHOR..290

Introduction

Welcome!

Hello amazing author-to-be,

Congratulations on taking a courageous step toward making your dreams come true—you are on the verge of becoming a self-published author. Very soon you will be holding your book, just like this one, in your own hands!

How to Use This Book

This book is designed to be used as workbook to follow along with the 20-Minute Author 20-Day Challenge.

You can also use it as a stand-alone workbook at your own pace. If you want to go at a slower pace, we suggest taking one week to work through each chapter in depth.

To find out when the next 20-Minute Author Challenge is starting, head over to the info page at https://majacreative.com/the-20-minute-author-challenge/

01

Crystal Abundance

HOW TO ATTRACT WEALTH WITH NATURE'S GIFTS

WRITTEN BY YOU

HOW TO ATTRACT WEALTH
WITH NATURE'S GIFTS

Crystal

WRITTEN BY YOU

chapter one

THE 20-MINUTE
author

Welcome to Day 1 of your journey to becoming an author. Let's get straight into it because my goal is to help you get your book published and out into the world as soon as humanly possible!

STEP 1
speak your book into existence

Over the next 20 days, I want you to speak your book into existence—literally!

What I mean by that is instead of typing your book, I want you to record your voice and speak your book into your phone or computer. It might sound like an odd thing to do, but I want you to challenge yourself and give it a try.

Now, I've done the maths on this—the average person speaks at around 125 words per minute. If you talk for 20 minutes, you'll have 2500 words. Multiply that over 20 days, and you'll have 'spoken' 50,000 words. In comparison, we type roughly 40 words per minute, so the pace is much slower. Now if you didn't know, the average book is around 50,000 words, which equates to around 200 pages.

If you talk for 20 minutes, you'll have 2500 words.

When you break it down into bite sized pieces, doesn't it seem more achievable and less overwhelming than being asked to come up with a 50,000-word manuscript?

Another benefit of speaking your book instead of typing is that you come across more natural and conversational, which will give your book more personality and capture your true voice.

One of my favourite ways to record my voice is to use an app called REV, where you can record your voice straight from your phone and then send it off to get it transcribed. The process usually takes only a few hours and costs around a dollar per minute at the time of writing. There are many paid transcribing apps that you can discover online, so hunt around for one that suits your needs best.

Another option if you're on a computer is to open up a new Microsoft Word document, go to 'Edit', and select 'Start dictation' from the bottom of the menu. The words will appear right in front of you as you speak, so if you want, you can make edits to your document instantly after you finish speaking.

You can also record your book manuscript on your phone or computer as a voice memo and then get it transcribed by your virtual assistant, or you can send the recording once finished to a transcription service such as REV.

STEP 2:
make a commitment

Now that you've got your head wrapped around speaking your book into existence, the most important next step is to commit.

You really have to commit to working on your book and taking on this challenge every single day. You have to commit to recording your book every day for at least 20 minutes.

The best way to make a commitment is to schedule it in your calendar.

Now I'm one of those people that loves to get all the really challenging but important things out of the way first thing in the morning. I exercise, meditate, and journal shortly after I wake up, and now I have added book creation as part of my morning routine. This ensures that I spend at least 20 minutes working on my book before any meetings, distractions, or obligations get in my way.

So, get your calendar out now, whether that's on your phone, your computer, or a physical paper calendar or planner, and schedule 20 minutes each day to work on your book.

Your goal is to create a consistent habit around writing your book. In order to create a new habit that you can stick to, I recommend scheduling your book creation time at the same time every day.

If you have to get up 20 minutes earlier to make time for your book, so be it—you will thank yourself later.

Now, your most creative time may not be morning. Many people have a creative peak in the afternoon or evening. Your goal is to pick a time that you know will be the EASIEST for you to stick to—a time when

Your goal is to create a consistent habit around writing your book.

nothing else will get in the way. You're looking for a path of least resistance. So, what is the best time for you? Fill out your commitment pledge below and schedule it into your calendar now.

commitment pledge

SCHEDULE YOUR BOOK WRITING AND CREATION TIME IN YOUR CALENDAR!

I .... commit to working on
     YOUR NAME

my book for 20 minutes per day.

Starting from .... at ....
                    DATE   TIME

Signed ....
                   YOUR SIGNATURE

STEP 3
track your progress

The last step in this process is to keep yourself accountable and track your progress. The most satisfying thing about a challenge is crossing off each day as you move one step closer to completing your book. Tracking your steady progress makes you want to keep going, and you will feel amazing when you see your achievement and how far you've come at the end.

I'm a visual person, so I love doing this physically—I have a large mirror in my office where I write out the 20 days with some colourful window markers. I take great pleasure in crossing off each day as I am doing the challenge.

You can do the same at home on a piece of paper, a chalkboard, a whiteboard, a mirror, a window, or you can use the Progress Calendar I have included in this book to chart your progress daily.

I love seeing my progress physically in front of me—it is a reminder to keep going every day—but I also love technology. One of the best ways to track your progress in our modern age is to use a habit-tracking app, such as Strides.

Strides allows you to input a goal (write a book) and a goal streak (20 days), and it gives you daily prompts and reminders that help you work toward your goal. We use this app in the 20-Minute Author community to track progress and share screenshots of where we are at with our books.

There are many habit tracking apps available, so download the one that suits you best. Your goal is to record and track your progress daily, allowing you to stay focused and accountable until you finish your book.

chapter one
inspired actions

1) SPEAK

Download REV (www.rev.com) or use any other voice-recording tool and speak the first sentence of your book. I don't care what it is, just say the first few words. Once you have recorded your first sentence, go immediately into your next few sentences. It doesn't matter if these sentences don't sound right to you, or if you feel that they are not in the right order. Just start speaking. You can always edit this content later!

2) COMMIT

Schedule 20 minutes a day into your calendar to work on your book. Make this a daily habit.

3) TRACK

Track your progress daily. Use our Progress Calendar to track your daily progress or download a progress tracking app like Strides (www.stridesapp.com) for digital daily reminders.

4) PROGRESS CALENDAR

Use this Progress Calendar to track the progress on your book daily. We've included a few extra pages if you want to continue past the 20 days. My team and I have found that it takes 20 days to complete a rough draft of your book and another two to three rounds to get your book edited and ready for publication.

the 20 minute author
progress calendar

01 02 03 04

05 06 07 08

09 10 11 12

13 14 15 16

17 18 19 20

the 20 minute author
progress calendar

01 02 03 04

05 06 07 08

09 10 11 12

13 14 15 16

17 18 19 20

the 20 minute author
progress calendar

01 02 03 04

05 06 07 08

09 10 11 12

13 14 15 16

17 18 19 20

ATTRACT WEALTH
WITH NATURE'S GIFTS

Crystal Abundance

WRITTEN BY YOU

MASTER YOUR MIND

RAPID TRANSFORMATIONAL THERAPY

Transform your thoughts with healing sounds

YOUR NAME HERE

02

RAPID TRANSFORMATIONAL THERAPY

MASTER YOUR MIND

Transform your thoughts with healing sounds

YOUR NAME HERE

MASTER YOUR MIND

TRANSFORMATIONAL THERAPY

Transform your thoughts with healing

YOUR NAME HERE

chapter two

MINDSET HACKS TO BANISH IMPOSTOR
syndrome

Let's talk about one of the biggest blocks that can stop you in your tracks when it comes to working on your book—your mindset. But firstly, a word of caution — don't skip this chapter! Many of the authors we work with are coaches and consultants in the health and wellness industry who are actively teaching others about mindset. If this is you, you may feel like I am preaching to the converted and may feel tempted to skim past this section. Don't.

Take the time to assess your own thoughts, beliefs and mindset about writing your book and becoming an author. You may not even be aware that you too might have some limiting beliefs and fears and may need to master your mind to remove any blocks. Explore this section and see what comes up for you.

STEP 1
confront your fear

When you apply for my 20-Minute Author Challenge, I ask all members a couple of questions before they join, including:

'What is your biggest challenge that is stopping you from creating your book?'

Many members mention that their own self-doubt and fears are some of their biggest challenges. Some of the responses I receive include comments like:

- 'I'm stopping myself'.
- 'It's me'.
- 'I'm filled with fear and self-doubt that my book won't be any good'.
- 'I think it's my own bullshit excuses'.

STEP 2
challenge your impostor syndrome

If you're reading this book, you might realise that you're having fears and doubts about your book. Just like you, and like many creatives, I sometimes suffer from what is commonly called 'Impostor Syndrome'. I too have thought to myself things like, 'Who am I to write a book?' 'Is anyone even going to read this, let alone buy it?' 'What are they going to say when they read this?' 'What if it isn't any good?'

Impostor Syndrome is the feeling that you are a fraud. It is the fear that you're somehow underqualified or inadequate to carry out a task—such as writing and publishing a book—and that you're going to be exposed. Basically, it's a limiting belief that is rooted in fear and self-doubt. Impostor Syndrome can lead to writer's block, where you feel like you can't write because you're frozen in a mindset of not being good enough.

> *Impostor Syndrome can lead to writer's block, where you feel like you can't write because you're frozen in a mindset of not being good enough.*

Now, the good news is that you're not alone in this—many famous authors suffer from Impostor Syndrome. The even better news is that there are many modalities that you can use to erase these fears and thoughts from your mind.

So how do you do this? The first step is to acknowledge your thoughts, and the second step is to examine them. Sit down today in a quiet spot with this workbook and have a think. What are some of these fears that you are having? Where do you think they stem from?

STEP 3
mind your mindset

My message to you, my dear soon-to-be author, is that the world NEEDS your book! Your book doesn't have to be perfect. None of us were born with the skills to become a best-selling author or to know how to write properly. Every best-selling author in the world had the experience of being a first-time author. They have all been where you are now.

My advice to you is to keep going with your book, and don't let these fears stop you. You have knowledge, expertise, and a story to tell. When your book is published, it will make an impact on the world in ways that you can't predict.

Now, if you stick with me over the next 20 days and keep reading this book, I will show you some strategies that you can use to combat some of these fears. You and your book are here to serve the world, so keep going and don't let these fears stop you. There is somebody out there whose life will be changed when they read your book.

STEP 4
explore your modalities

There are many modalities that you can use to eradicate these thoughts and fears from your mind. I'm going to share some of the modalities that I personally use to work on my mindset.

Hypnotherapy & Rapid Transformational Therapy

I am a big believer in both hypnotherapy and RTT, and I have worked extensively with a number of coaches and therapists in these modalities to shift my mindset. Hypnotherapy allows you to get to the root cause of your issues, which often stem from childhood experience. A qualified hypnotherapist helps you develop a different dialogue in your mind, which is then recorded as an audio. I listen to my audios twice a day to help me re-program my thoughts and beliefs about myself, and this has been the most effective and powerful way of transforming my thoughts and behaviours.

Neurolinguistic Programming

NLP is one of my favourite modalities for rapidly changing my inner dialogue. It allows me to eradicate fears and negative thoughts that continue to come up. I work with NLP coaches who help me clear unhealthy patterns as they arise.

Emotional Freedom Technique

EFT is a modality developed by Roger Callahan. He discovered that tapping different meridians can release stored emotions. Brad Yates is a guru of EFT, and he has a free YouTube video specifically on impostor

The world needs your book!

syndrome (https://youtu.be/mz2kDDJUok4). I recommend watching it to learn how to quickly release fear and self-doubt.

Affirmations

One of my favourite ways to work on my mindset is to use affirmations and visualization. I often journal first thing in the morning. I picture a goal that I have, such as becoming a published author, and then I write these goals as 'I am' statements, such as 'I am a published author'. I keep writing 'I am' statements until I have filled a page. I want you to consider doing this today. Grab a piece of paper and think about your goal. Do you want to become a best-selling author? Do you want to write a book so that you become a famous speaker? How many people do you want to impact with your book?

Write each goal as an 'I am' statement and put it somewhere that you can see it every single day. I have done this before with many different goals. One of my biggest goals was adjusting my beliefs about who I am, so I even had 'I am enough' on my mirror for a good twelve months before I started to own that belief. Writing these affirmations rewires your brain. As you see these statements every day and say them out loud to yourself, the next thing you know, you will start believing these statements. When you change your beliefs, they become your reality, so try it today!

Vision Board & Visualisation

If you're a visual person like me, I recommend creating a vision board for writing your book. You can do this on Pinterest, or you can cut out pictures and quotes and glue them onto a physical board. Imagine your life as an author and make sure to include your goals in your vision board. If you want to become a speaker, where are you going to get speaking gigs? If you want to create a podcast, who do you want to collab with first? Just include all of it and keep it in front of you daily so your vision can come to life.

chapter two
inspired actions

1) WRITE YOUR NEGATIVE BELIEFS

Write down your negative beliefs. Make a list of all the negative thoughts and beliefs that are circulating in your head about becoming a published author. Keep going until you feel like you've listed them all. Examine each one. Next to it, write where you think that thought or belief comes from.

2) WRITE A POSITIVE COUNTERPOINT

Write an opposite, positive statement underneath each negative belief that you have written above. For example: Rewrite 'I'll never finish writing this book' as 'It will be easy for me to complete this book'. Rewrite 'I can't do this' as 'I know I can do this'. Start owning these new beliefs.

OLD BELIEF	NEW BELIEF
....	....
....	....
....	....
....	....
....	....
....	....
....	....
....	....
....	....
....	....
....	....
....	....
....	....
....	....
....	....
....	....

3) KEEP MOVING FORWARD THROUGH FEAR

Your book doesn't have to be perfect. Keep going with your book and don't let your fears stop you. Write 'I am unstoppable' on your bathroom mirror where you will see it every single day.

4) INCORPORATE SELF-DEVELOPMENT MODALITIES

1. Circle which modalities you would like to try to clear negative beliefs or list your own.

   Hypnotherapy & Rapid Transformational Therapy

   Neurolinguistic Programming

   Emotional Freedom Technique

   Affirmations

   Vision Board & Visualisation

....

....

....

....

....

....

....

....

....

....

2. Write your 'I am' statement and affirmations—you can borrow some of mine.

I am unstoppable
I am a published author
The universe has my back
I am creative and successful
Writing my book is quick and easy
I am intelligent and clever
My book is a best-seller
I am a wealthy woman
My book is an inspiration
I am breezing through this book project
I know I can do this
My book makes a positive impact in the world
It's so easy to write my next chapter
I make time for my writing every day
Everythig is always working out for me
The words just flow easily out of me
My book is valuable to those who need to read it
I am a brilliant writer
I have raving fans and five star reviews
My book creates wealth and abundance
for me and my family

3. Create a vision board for your book and life as a published author or write out your vision.

03

chapter three

START WITH
your why

Simon Sinek wrote an amazing book called *Start With Why*. In it, he suggests that people don't buy what you do, they buy why you do it.

STEP 1:
ask yourself why

Have a think about this idea today in the context of your book. Take a step back, and ask yourself—why do you want to become an author? Why are you writing your book? What is the purpose of your book? What is the intention that you want to achieve with your book?

- Is writing your book your end goal in itself? Will you be happy when you've completed it and ticked it off the bucket list?
- Do you have a unique story that you want to share with the world?
- Do you want to use your book as a lead magnet for your business to attract dream clients and customers?
- Are you writing your book because you want to raise your profile, establish your personal brand, and increase your credibility?
- Perhaps you want to be like one of my clients who wanted to become an international speaker, and your book is a vehicle to launch you into that platform?
- Do you dream of becoming a well-known authorpreneur and make a living from writing multiple books?

STEP 2
brainstorm your reasons why

Brainstorm these ideas today and come up with the one that resonates most with you. There are no right or wrong answers here. Check in with yourself, close your eyes, listen to your heart, and think about the core purpose of why you're writing your book—the answer might surprise you!

Why do you want to become an author?

Once you get clear on your why, you are more likely to achieve the outcome you want, because you are defining a clear goal. When you know your purpose, it's much easier to achieve it.

It is important to know the core reasons within you of your why, to know why you have been gifted with the idea of your book. It will help with your author branding and marketing. Remember, people don't buy what you do, they buy why you do it.

STEP 3
use your why to write your book

Many authors have multiple books up their sleeve. If you have a few book ideas, but you're not sure which one to go with, be careful that this indecision doesn't manifest as a block that can stop you from becoming an author.

Move forward fast by narrowing down your ideas. Write out your book idea list and have a think about each one. Ask yourself why you want to write each book—how does it link in with your bigger why? You'll quickly find the reasons that resonate the most with you.

I know I have at least three books that I want to write in the near future, and I thought that a book about branding would be the first book I ever wrote. However, when I took a step back and went through this process myself, I realised that it was more important for me to get this book out as fast as I could—and here you are reading it!

Becoming an author was something that I committed to achieving in 2020, so I chose to write the book that I had researched the most and felt ready to finish quickly with the least resistance. This book explores a topic that I am passionate about. It resonates with my bigger purpose, which is to use creativity to make a positive impact in the world. Writing this book was also a strategic move—it made the most sense to help me grow my business and show off my creativity. My other books just need a bit more 'baking' in my brain before I publish.

So, what's your big why? Why are YOU writing your amazing book?

chapter three
inspired actions

1) DEFINE YOUR WHY

In order to measure success, you first have to be able to define it. Explore some of the reasons why you are writing your book.

....
....
....
....
....
....
....
....
....
....
....
....
....
....
....
....
....
....
....
....

2) BRAINSTORM YOUR WHY

Brain dump all your book ideas and ask yourself these four questions:

1. Why do I want to become an author?

   ....
   ....
   ....
   ....
   ....

2. Why am I writing this book?

   ....
   ....
   ....
   ....
   ....

3. What is the purpose of this book?

   ....
   ....
   ....
   ....
   ....
   ....

4. What do I want this book to achieve in my life?

....

....

....

....

....

3) USE YOUR WHY TO WRITE YOUR BOOK

Narrow down your top three book ideas and pick one. Go with your gut (along with a healthy dose of logic).

....

....

....

....

....

....

....

....

....

....

....

04

YOUR NAME HERE

POLAND
THE HEART OF EUROPE

chapter four

DEVELOP YOUR IDEAL
reader profile

When it comes to writing a book, we can often get stuck in the creation mode and think a lot about the structure—such as how to write, the author voice or what's going to be in the next chapter—and we overlook an essential element, which is to think about your audience, i.e. the people who will be reading your book.

four things you need to know before you start writing

I know that you're not here to create a book just to do an exercise. I know that you want to write a book because you want to serve and help people. The thing is, you can't be all things to all people. The more specific you can get about who your book is written for, the more successful your book will be, and the more successful the marketing of your book will be.

When I start working with my clients to design their books and their book covers, we do an in-depth exercise to develop their Ideal Reader profile. This process helps you get inside your readers heads, hearts, and minds to understand who they are. What is it that they need, and how is this book going to help them?

> *The more specific you can get about who your book is written for, the more successful your book will be*

This becomes even more important if you're in business and your book has the additional purpose to attract soulmate clients and grow your business. If that's the case, you also have to think about the end consumer—someone who will not only buy and read your book but will interact with your business and your other offers.

Having an in-depth understanding of your audience is one of the most important things you can do when you're first writing your book. It will help you develop your key concepts as you write the content of your book, and it will also assist with developing your marketing strategy.

Essentially, there are four things that you really need to know about your audience before you start writing and marketing your book. Let's explore the information you need to gather about your audience.

STEP 1
who do you want to serve with your book?

Who is your book speaking to? Your book is a communication tool—you are having a dialogue with somebody through your book, so you have to ask yourself, who do you want to serve with this book? Who do you want to talk to, and will they want to communicate with you?

You can answer this question more broadly by developing their demographic profile and starting to delve deeper into who they are. This is your opportunity to get specific about who this person is, and the more specific you can be, the more targeted you can be with your book branding, design, and marketing.

Who Is Your Ideal Reader?

- How old are they?
- Male or female?
- Where do they work? What is their career/occupation?
- How much money do they make?
- Where do they live? Which postcode?
- What kind of house do they live in?
- What kind of car do they drive?
- Are they married, single, coupled, or divorced?
- Do they have kids? Pets? How big is their family?
- What is their level of education? Did they finish highschool? University?
- What do they do in their spare time?
- What are their life goals and aspirations?
- What is on their bucket list?
- Where can you find them? Are they on Instagram, Facebook, LinkedIn, or Twitter?

How Would You Describe Your Ideal Reader?

What is their personality like? Pick five to ten adjectives that would best describe your ideal reader. Try not to overthink this and quickly list

The more specific you can be, the more targeted you can be with your book branding, design and marketing.

the ones that first come to mind. E.g. Smart, stressed, busy, frustrated, ambitious, etc.

Imagine a specific person that would want to read your book. Maybe this is someone you know, such as a client of your business. Give your ideal reader a name and picture them in your mind's eye. This is the person that you are speaking to when you write your book.

What Are Your Ideal Reader's Values?

This is an important insight into who they are and what their belief systems are. Your book needs to resonate with your ideal reader's values—e.g., are they career driven, family focused, work hard play hard, or a unique combination?

STEP 2
how will my ideal reader benefit from my offer?

Now that you've started to paint a picture of who your ideal reader is, dig deeper and think about whether this is someone that is going to benefit from what you have to offer—will their life improve from reading your book, and if they continue to engage with you, will they want to partake in your other offers, workshops, or programs?

What Is Their Story?

Think about your ideal reader's typical day. What are some of the challenges they are facing? What are the specific problems that you can help them solve? What are their pain points?

What Do They Need From Your Book?

Your readers are seeking information—what is it exactly that they want and need from your book? What do they need from your book? What do they expect to find when they read your book?

What Is The Benefit Of Your Book?

How does your book solve their problems and pain points? How does your book address some of challenges your readers are experiencing? What is the outcome that they get from reading your book?

What Makes Your Book Unique?

What makes your book unique compared to others that your ideal reader might encounter about this topic? How does your book meet and exceed their needs, wants, and expectations? What is something extra that your book can provide them that they are not expecting?

STEP 3
is my ideal reader willing and able to work with me?

You have to go further and think beyond the person who is going to buy and read your book. Think about the person who is going to take action after reading your book. This applies to you if you're in business and your book is designed to introduce your audience to your other programs and services—will they be interested in your offer? Will they be able to engage with you in a meaningful way? Is this person going to be able to afford your offer, and are they going to be willing to pay for it?

STEP 4
what experience do i want my reader to have with my book?

Reading is an experience, so think about how you want your ideal reader to feel when they are reading your book?

If they sign on to work with you further after reading your book, what experience do you want them to have with you and your brand, company, or business? What kind of testimonial or review would you like your ideal reader to leave for you on Amazon?

chapter four
inspired actions

1) BE SPECIFIC

When it comes to developing your ideal reader profile, the more specific you can be, the easier it will be to connect and communicate with your audience through your book and through your marketing.

Don't make the book for you, and don't make the book for everyone—be laser specific without fear that someone is going to miss out. Keeping this information about your ideal reader on hand will help develop your marketing assets and key messaging for your book, and when your ideal reader hears your message, they will be drawn to your book.

1. How old are they?

   ....
   ....
   ....
   ....
   ....

2. Male or female?

   ....
   ....
   ....
   ....

3. Where do they work? What is their career/occupation?

....
....
....
....
....

4. How much money do they make?

....
....
....
....
....

5. Where do they live? Which postcode?

....
....
....
....
....

6. What kind of house do they live in?

....
....
....

7. What kind of car do they drive?

....

....

....

8. Are they married, single, coupled, or divorced?

....

....

....

....

9. Do they have kids? Pets? How big is their family?

....

....

....

....

10. What is their level of education? Did they finish high-school? University?

....

....

....

....

....

11. What do they do in their spare time?

....

....

....

....

....

12. What are their life goals and aspirations?

....

....

....

....

....

13. What is on their bucket list?

....

....

....

....

14. Where can you find them? Are they on Instagram, Facebook, LinkedIn, or Twitter?

....

....

....

....

2) HOW WILL MY IDEAL READER BENEFIT FROM MY OFFER?

1. What is their story? What are some of their challenges?

....
....
....
....
....
....
....
....

2. What do they need from your book?

....
....
....
....
....
....
....
....
....
....
....

3. What is the benefit of your book?

....
....
....
....
....
....
....
....
....

4. What makes your book unique?

....
....
....
....
....
....
....
....
....

3) IS MY IDEAL READER WILLING AND ABLE TO WORK WITH ME?

4) WHAT EXPERIENCE DO I WANT MY READER TO HAVE WITH MY BOOK?

Cuddly Cats

Best breeds for apartment living

AUTHOR NAME HERE

05

chapter five

JOIN THE 20-MINUTE AUTHOR
20-day challenge

As mentioned in the beginning, this workbook has been designed to go hand-in-hand with the 20-Minute Author 20-Day Challenge.

STEP 1
sign up for the challenge

If you haven't done so already, sign up for the Challenge. We will we work through the exercises together with daily videos from me to guide you through the entire process.

STEP 2
join our community of like-minded authors

When you join the Challenge you'll get instant access tour growing community of authors in my private Facebook group, where you will get to meet and mingle with like-minded souls who are also working on their books. It is a sacred space for you and your book.

STEP 3
get personal guidance from me

I'll share my journey of creating this book and the best tips on writing and mindset from my panel of experts. I'll also reveal strategies, interviews, and case studies from past clients who are now published authors. You'll have the opportunity to get personal support from me and my creative team to help you publish your book.

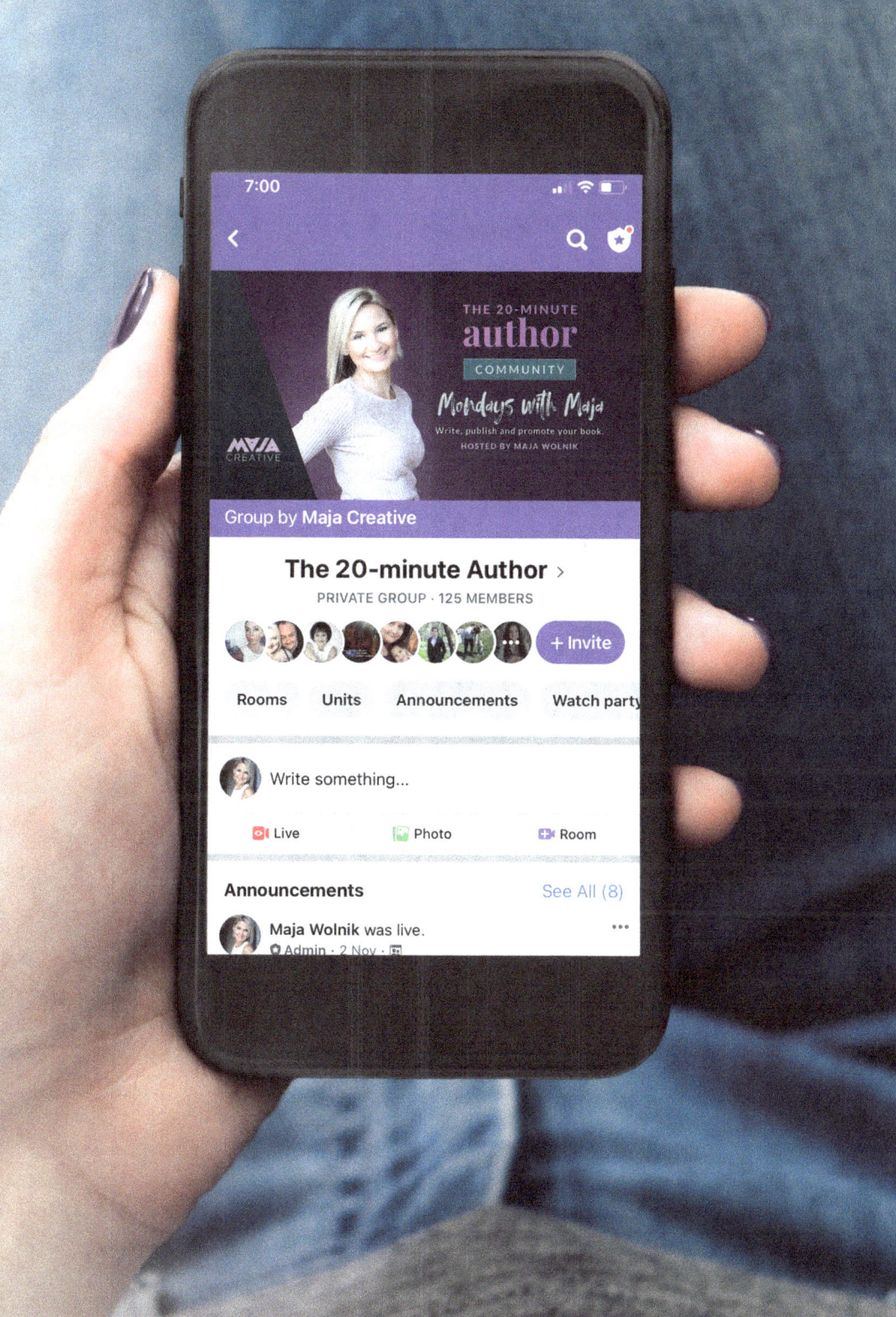

chapter five
inspired actions

JOIN THE 20-MINUTE AUTHOR 20-DAY CHALLENGE.

Follow the link below to register and find out the dates of our next live challenge!

https://majacreative.com/the-20-minute-author-challenge/

WHAT OUR COMMUNITY HAS TO SAY...

I'm genuinely enthused and my imagination is running wild. I'm crunching through the challenge fast. The Pinterest board thing in Day 11 is quite helpful.
- Scott

I am struggling with my second book but the tips are really helping me.
- Julie

Thank you! I have been stuck in getting started and I spent time tonight speaking my book. The wheels are finally turning.
- Garnet

Thank you great tips.
- Sarina

Thank you for sharing that we can record directly into Rev - I did not know that. An excellent insight that recording your book creates more natural and authentic content.
- Janet

I love the idea of speaking the book.
- Paul'

This is some great advice. I definitely over think whilst typing.
- Lea

Thanks for the tip. I didn't know it existed & loving the idea.
- Katherine

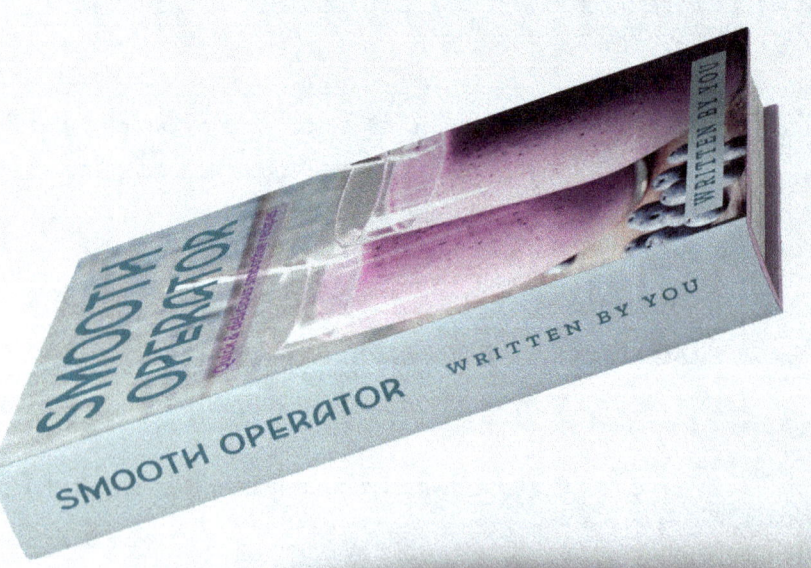

06

chapter six

GET YOUR
**book
chapters**
SORTED

Let's check in. By now, you have identified your ideal reader, you've started using voice-to-text to speak your book into existence, and you're beginning to work through your chapters. At this point, you might be wondering—how exactly do I do this? How do I set up a better structure so that I'm not just speaking randomly into my voice recorder?

are you mumbling random thoughts into your voice recorder?

If you're getting a little stuck with 'writing' today, I want to share a simple mind mapping exercise that will help you visually organise your thoughts, structure your chapters, and flesh out your book.

I used my iPad for this exercise, but you can also use a piece of paper and a pen, or you can do it on a whiteboard. If you love tech, then I highly recommend you download an app called Mindly (www.mindlyapp.com) for this.

STEP 1
map your book's theme

I want you write what your book is about in the centre of the page. Don't worry about your book title or anything like that for now. In my example below, I have simply written 'A Book about Books'.

STEP 2
map your book's topics

Around it, start writing down the topics that you want to cover in your book. Don't overthink this; instead, brain dump your top-level topics. They don't have to be in any particular order; just put down whatever comes to mind first.

STEP 3
map your book's headings

Underneath each topic, put down a couple of bullet points of the key things you want to say about that topic. These are your headings and subheadings.

These topics and headings are loosely going to become the chapters and sections of your book. Pick one that feels the easiest right now and begin speaking about each bullet point into your voice recorder.

my mind map

In my example, I have listed ten key topics that I wanted to cover in my workbook about books, and I've jotted some key ideas that I wanted to flesh out about each topic.

As you can see, this is a really simple and fast way to organise your thoughts into book chapters and start to develop some structure to your book. Don't worry too much about the order of them now or what you will call each chapter. You can always change that later during the editing process. Keep moving forward and start speaking about the first topic that comes to mind. Before you know it, you will be on a roll. You can assemble all your text together later once you've transcribed your voice-to-text.

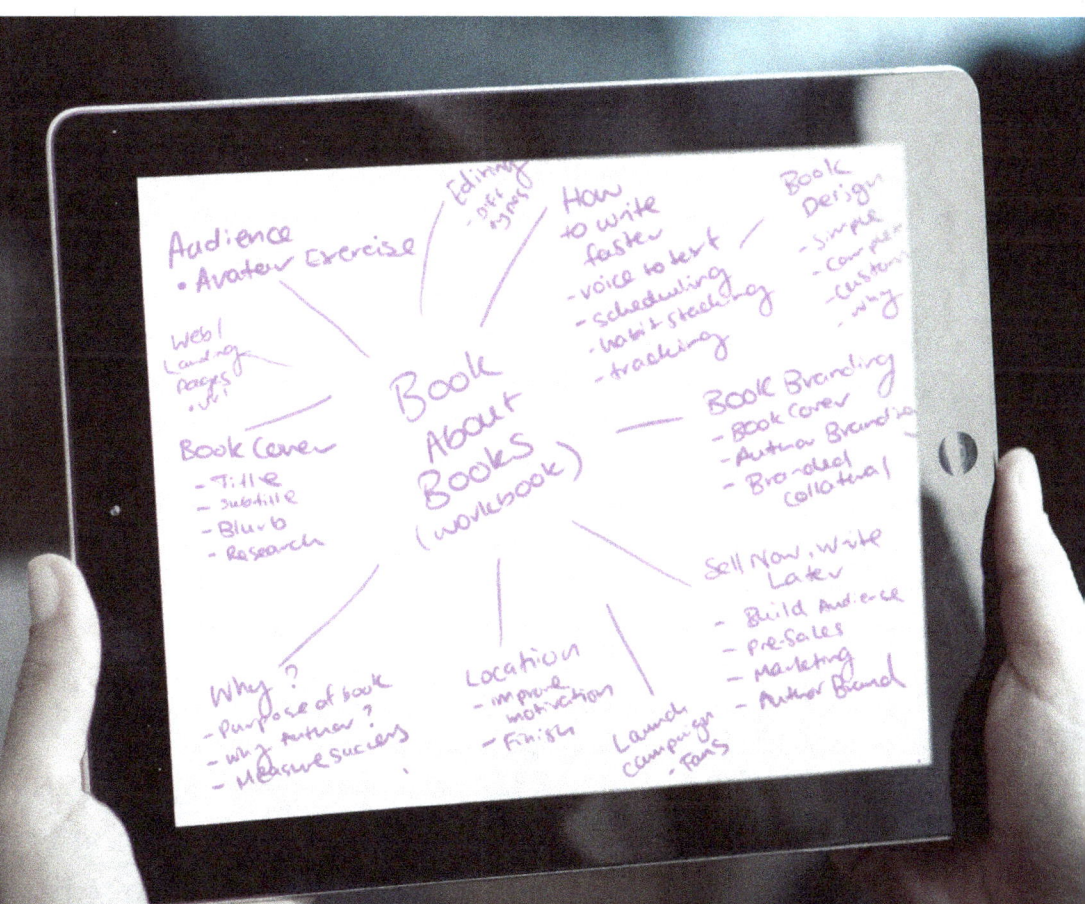

chapter six
inspired actions

BRAIN DUMP AND MIND MAP YOUR BOOK TOPICS

To recap, today's inspired action is to do a brain dump and mind map your book topics, which will then become your book chapters.

....
....
....
....
....
....
....
....
....
....
....
....
....
....
....
....
....

DRAW YOUR BOOK MIND MAP HERE:

07

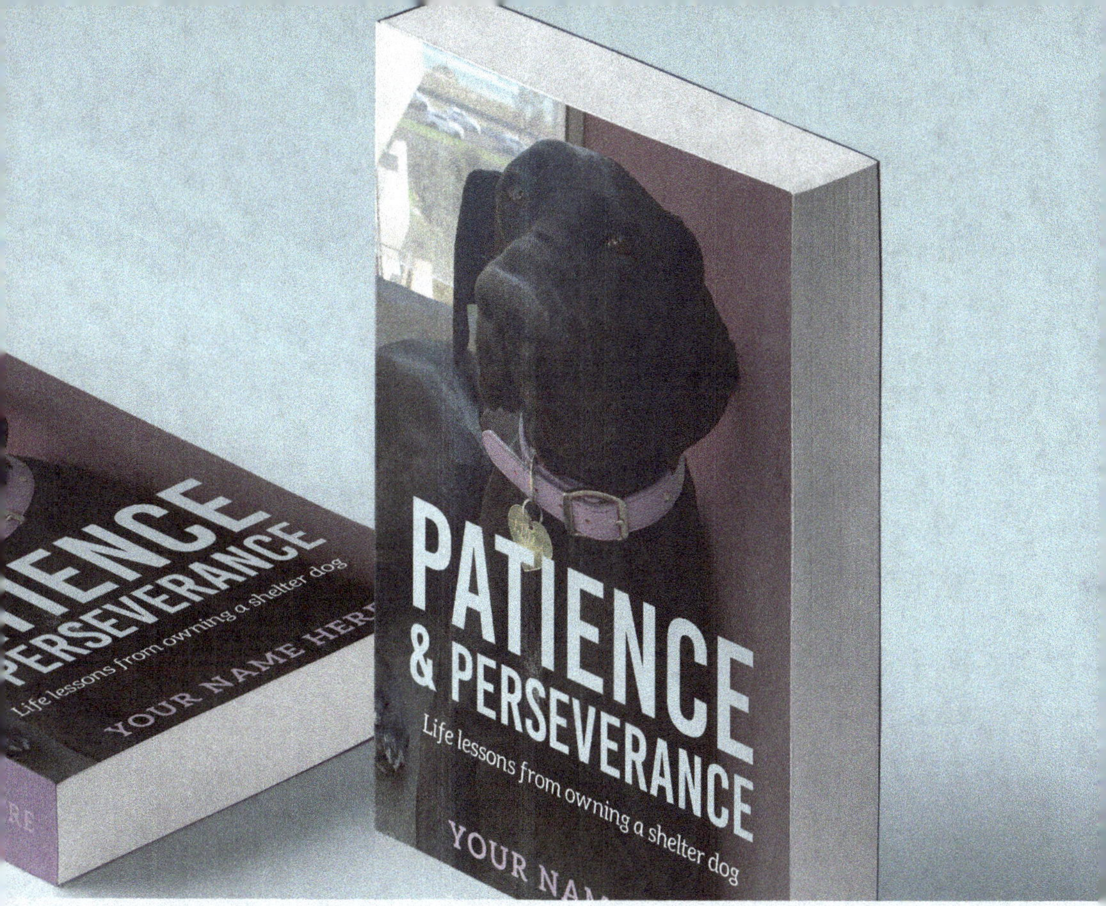
PATIENCE
& PERSEVERANCE
Life lessons from owning a shelter dog
YOUR NAME HERE

PATIENCE
& PERSEVERANCE
Life lessons from owning a shelter dog
YOUR NAME HERE

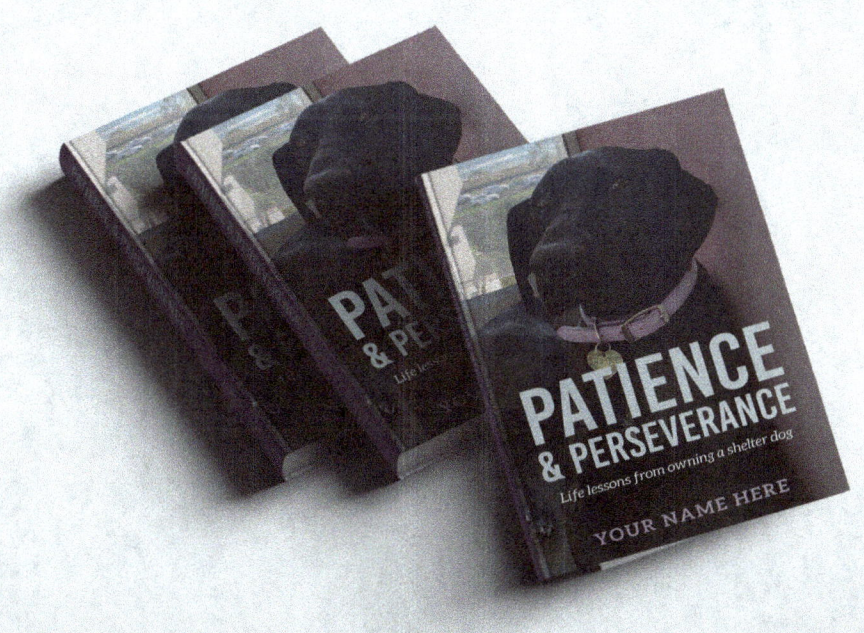

chapter seven

HOW TO SELECT A BEST-SELLING
book title

Your title and subtitle are both essential when it comes to marketing and selling your book. You want to select a book title that will connect with your readers. There are seven elements that I want you to consider when selecting your best-selling book title.

STEP 1
find out what's in it for your ideal reader

Go back to your ideal reader profile and have a think about what kind of title would appeal to your audience. When someone looks at your book, they are going to think, 'What's in it for me?' Your book title should be able to answer that question immediately.

STEP 2
keep it short and simple

Your book title should be short and simple, like a popular hashtag. You want it to be easy to spell, memorable enough to search for online, and short enough to create a custom URL and landing page for your book.

Stick to four words or less when it comes to your book title. You also want to make sure that your book title is easy to pronounce—you don't want you or anyone else getting tongue tied when talking about your book. You're going to be mentioning your book many times on video, in interviews, and on podcasts when you're promoting it, so you want to make it memorable and easy to say.

STEP 3
make it memorable

Your book title should be easy to remember, so try to create something catchy and intriguing. Think of a way that your title could be unusual, provocative, or a play on words—you want to stand out from all the other books that are in your category or about your topic.

STEP 4
summarise one concept

Your title should reflect the whole concept of your book. If you could summarise what your book is about in a few words, what would that be? Look for a creative, memorable way of describing your book in four words or less. See if that can form your book title.

STEP 5
elaborate with a subtitle

Your subtitle is the line underneath your book. It helps elaborate on your title and further describes what your book is about. It should also be simple, short, and sharp, and it should drive the core message of your book home. Your subtitle should immediately tell the reader what kind of results your book will give them.

STEP 6
scope out the competition

Go into Amazon or any other online book retailer and search for similar books in your category. Imagine what your ideal reader would search for if they were looking for books like yours.

Once you do this search, you will get an idea of the types of titles that are doing well. It is also important to do this search because you don't want to have a title that is similar to someone else's in your category.

STEP 7
take note of keywords

Keywords are an important part of your title creation. Even if you develop a catchy title, your book might be hard to find in search engines if it doesn't include the keywords that people are searching for. If you can't include keywords in your book title, make sure you try to include them in your subtitle or at the very least, in your book description.

chapter seven
inspired actions

SELECT A BEST-SELLING BOOK TITLE

Consider the above seven elements when brainstorming and selecting your bestselling book title. The first step is to brain dump all the book title ideas that you have. I don't want you to discount any—jot them all down so you can get them out of your head, then narrow down your list to two favorites. Do the same thing when selecting your subtitle. If you're in the group or going through the challenge, share your titles in the group so we can vote as a community.

1. Research titles and subtitles in your category on Amazon. List any that you like.

....
....
....
....
....
....
....
....
....
....

2. Brainstorm your titles—just write down all that come to mind; don't dismiss any.

....

....

....

....

....

....

....

....

....

....

....

....

....

....

....

....

....

....

3. Narrow down to two options.

....

....

....

4. Brainstorm your subtitles—just write down all that come to mind; don't dismiss any.

....

....

....

....

....

....

....

....

....

....

....

....

....

....

....

....

....

5. Narrow down to two options.

....

....

....

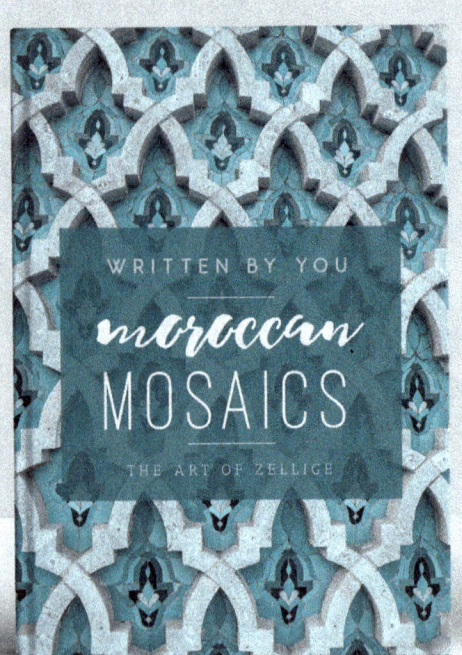

08

chapter eight

SECURE YOUR UNIQUE
book title

Once you've selected your book title (or you have a shortlist of your two favourites), make sure to secure it by purchasing the same domain name. This is essential when it comes to marketing your book. If you have come up with a catchy title, you'll be surprised how quickly some of those titles can be snapped up, especially if you're using specific keywords. Even if you haven't decided on your book title yet, you can purchase some of the ones on your shortlist, and you can always cancel your domain names later. Each domain name is approximately $20 per year.

STEP 1
make your branding consistent

When it's time to market your book, you'll want to drive traffic quickly and easily to your book. Having a unique URL with your book title is key. Now you might already have your own website, but you don't want to confuse your audience. Your book title should be the only thing they have to remember.

STEP 2
be strategic when purchasing your url

On a side note, be careful when you're searching for your URL, because I have found that some popular websites that offer domain names can get a bit sneaky. If they see that you are shopping for a unique URL, they often snap them up, park them, and then offer to you for resale with elevated prices. Don't let this happen to you. Once you find a domain name that works for your book, buy it quickly.

STEP 3
purchase multiple urls

I recommend purchasing multiple URLs for both your book title and your author name. This will help when you establish your personal brand, and it will give your readers multiple ways to find you online.

STEP 4
create your custom landing page

Once you secure the domain name for your book title, you will be able to create a custom landing page dedicated to your book. Your landing page will provide an opportunity for your audience to learn more about

The goal is to create a path of least resistance.

your book and about you as an author, and it will give them further information on where they can purchase your book. You want your readers to be able to purchase your book directly from your landing page, and you want to provide links to third party sites, such as Amazon. The goal is to create a path of least resistance. You don't want your audience to get lost along the way or have to remember multiple sites when shopping for your book.

chapter eight
inspired actions

SECURE YOUR BOOK TITLE URL

1. Seek out and purchase your book's domain name.

   ....
   ....
   ....

2. Consider purchasing multiple URLs to complete your branding.

   ....
   ....
   ....
   ....

3. Start planning the custom landing page for your book's website.

   ....
   ....
   ....
   ....
   ....
   ....

09

chapter nine

MOTIVATION
check-in

Checking in—how are you tracking with your book? If you're following the challenge, day seven through day nine can get notoriously challenging when it comes to staying committed. This is where your motivation can start to drop off. Perhaps you haven't done all of the exercises, or you have missed a couple of days. Perhaps distractions in your life have eaten into your writing time.

STEP 1
break through your motivation blocks

At the time of writing this book, the whole world was going through a global pandemic due to the Covid-19 coronavirus. Not only were there heartbreaking death statistics around the world, but we had major restrictions to our normal way of life and unfathomable economic impacts to every sector globally. Hopefully, if you're reading this now, the worst of it is over.

When I first started writing my book and hosting the 20-Day Challenge in December 2019, my home country of Australia was hit with one of the worst bushfire seasons in history. The country was literally burning. It was a truly scary time when smoke filled the air, our wildlife was dying, and people lost their homes. Both those events impacted me personally and professionally, yet I knew however bad things got, I had to keep moving forward. In order to maintain my momentum, I had to work on my motivation.

> *There is always going to be something that will potentially stop you in your tracks.*

STEP 2
keep going no matter what

Every day we deal with different challenges and events on the news that affect us. My message to you is that there is always going to be something that will potentially stop you in your tracks. Whether that's something happening in the news or something happening in your personal life, there will be obstacles that can get in the way of you working on your book—if you let them.

If you've fallen off the bandwagon, there is no better day than today to dust yourself off and just keep going. Get back on the horse! It doesn't matter if you've written only one sentence, or if you haven't even started your book. Today is a good day to start again.

STEP 3
the world needs your book

I genuinely believe that the world needs your book, now more than ever. There is someone out there that needs to hear your message—they need your knowledge and expertise, and they need to hear your story. Don't let anything stop you; you can always find reasons to shelve your book, so instead look for reasons to keep writing. Think of your ideal reader, the person who needs your book, and speak your book directly to them. Dust yourself off, recommit to the challenge, recommit to yourself, and find that 20 minutes in your day to work on your book. I promise, you will not regret it.

STEP 4
no more bullshit excuses

So, what's stopping you? Do you need to do your laundry? Or do you have to help your kids with their homework? Is your spouse or significant other asking for your time, and you don't have the headspace to write? Perhaps you're tired, don't have time, or just feel uninspired to work on your book?

Write out a list of everything that is stopping you from working on your book. Take a deep breath, and then examine your list of bullshit excuses. Dig deeper—some of these come up as real-life obstacles but are masked in deeper insecurities, like fear of being seen, fear of failure, or even fear of success. Check in with yourself—if you need to go back to Chapter 2 and work on your mindset, please do so. Review your list, and next to each 'reason', write how you can change it around and make it work so that you can return to writing your book.

Your book is important—the world needs it—so make space for your book in your life. Search for what you have to change, let go of, or adjust to make you and your book a priority.

chapter nine
inspired actions

REDISCOVER YOUR MOTIVATION FOR WRITING YOUR BOOK

1. Write out your list of all the reasons you CAN'T work on your book. Reflect on each excuse.

2. Write a list of all the reasons you CAN work on your book, addressing each bullshit excuse.

....

....

....

....

....

....

....

....

....

....

....

....

....

....

....

3. Recommit to your book. List three things you need to change to make space for your book in your life.

....

....

....

....

10

THE 20-MINUTE author

STEP-BY-STEP WORKBOOK

Just 20-minutes per day!

Your custom roadmap to write, publish and promote your book.

MAJA WOLNIK

THE 20-MINUTE author

STEP-BY-STEP WORKBOOK

Your custom roadmap to write, publish and promote your book.

Just 20-minutes per day!

MAJA WOLNIK

chapter ten

START PROMOTING YOUR
book now

If you've reached this chapter, then your book really should be underway by now. Tick the boxes that you have accomplished so far!

☐ You have a clear understanding of who your ideal reader is.

☐ You have organised your thoughts into book chapters and are working through your manuscript.

☐ You've narrowed down your perfect book title.

☐ You've secured that book title by purchasing its unique domain name.

If you have achieved those key elements, then you have the perfect recipe to start promoting your book right now!

You might be thinking, 'But, I haven't finished writing my book yet!' That's okay. I want to plant this idea early so you can understand how to market your book while you write. I like to practice what I preach, so I want to share some ideas and behind the scenes of how I used these elements to build my audience and share the story of my book, creating buzz before my book was finished.

> *You have the perfect recipe to start promoting your book right now!*

STEP 1
book cover design

The first thing that my team and I did was to design my book cover. We will go in depth into book covers in later chapters because it is a crucial part of the marketing strategy; however, as you can see here, we designed the front, back, and spine ahead of time.

We used the same branding for the book cover as we did to promote the 20-Minute Author Challenge because this workbook goes hand in hand with the challenge, so it was important to have a unified look. That kind of consistency builds brand familiarity and brand recognition.

The cover design has been the key marketing element for this book, and I'll show you why.

THE 20-MINUTE author

STEP-BY-STEP WORKBOOK

Your custom roadmap to write, publish and promote your book.

Just 20-minutes per day!

MAJA WOLNIK

STEP 2
book mockups & photography

Once the book cover design was finalised, we were able to use that artwork to create some 3D looking mockup images of my book. As you can see in the examples below, we created some simple images of the book in different scenarios, angles, and backgrounds.

The book cover was also professionally printed and made into a real-life sample of my book.

I also took cell phone pictures of the book sample to use in my social media. I created a couple of cute little Boomerangs, and I took some natural shots of me holding the book.

You only need about six to ten images to get started. Using the sample cover design is the key element in beginning your book promotion journey.

Once you have a physical sample of your book, you can also organise a professional photoshoot if you want to create a series of high-quality shots that feature you and your book.

STEP 3
social media assets

Next, using the images and mockups of the book, we created social media assets to use on Facebook, LinkedIn, and Instagram. I used the images of the book to promote the 20-Minute Author 20-Day Challenge. As you can see in these examples, I started to lace my book into the marketing that I was already doing, and you can do the same with your book if it is relevant to your business.

There is one particularly effective image that I took myself with my iPhone. It shows me holding my book with my messy apartment in the background. This picture tells the story that even though you're busy, you just need to find 20 minutes per day in-between the messiness of life to become an author. I used this image for Facebook ads, which worked well for this challenge. Having this combination of professional images and quick and dirty selfies is an effective marketing strategy.

I decided to presell my book to get a feel for the market and see if there was interest in the book. My team created a series of assets in line with the 20-Minute Author branding to help sell the book, including breakout icons like 'Coming Soon', 'Preorder Now', and 'Book launching in 2020'. We created Facebook and LinkedIn banners, a suite of social media tiles, and FB and Instagram stories so that anyone coming to visit my pages would know that I was about to launch my book. All of the assets were linked to a dedicated landing page for my book.

> *You just need to find 20 minutes per day in-between the messiness of life to become an author.*

STEP 4
custom landing page

If you have secured your book URL, the best way to promote your book is to create a dedicated landing page. As you can see in my example, we used a clear, strong image of the book at the top of the landing page as an intro. I also held the printed book sample in an intro video to explain what the book is about.

The landing page tells your ideal readers how they will benefit from your book and shows them where they can purchase it. Here you can share more information about yourself as an author to build your credibility. Your landing page also allows you to collect the email addresses and names of interested readers. You want to start building a database of people who are likely to purchase your book.

I also used my landing page to invite people into my private Facebook Group—The 20-Minute Author—where they can receive more book publishing training videos, tips and strategies My landing page was linked to a shopping cart and allowed my audience to pre-order the book. There are many ways you can set up pre-orders and payment gateways on your landing page. Preselling your book is a simple strategy to get some cash flow for your book so you can fund it while you're still writing it.

My team and I can help you develop your landing page copy and your book mockup with our Ultimate Author Starter Kit package.

THE 20-MINUTE AUTHOR
write, publish and promote your book in easy, bite-sized steps

Become a published author in just 20-minutes per day. This step-by-step workbook by Maja Wolnik is your custom roadmap to launch your book, fast.

PRE-ORDER NOW

PRE-ORDER THE 20-MINUTE AUTHOR BOOK >>> ADD TO CART

A MESSAGE FROM THE AUTHOR

about the book
THE 20-MINUTE AUTHOR

Don't have time to write your book? The 20-minute Author is your custom roadmap to help you write, publish and promote your book in easy, bite-sized steps.

By allocating just 20-minutes per day to work on your book, you can follow the daily steps, tips and prompts to finally get your book started and finished, fast.

This workbook can be used along with the famous 20-minute Author 30-day Challenge, to which you can join and access here.

Use The 20-minute Author to launch your book, share your wisdom, leverage your expertise and build an additional income stream.

IN THIS WORKBOOK
you'll discover...

- Simple tech #hacks to finish your book fast and make it a daily habit
- How to launch and pre-sell your book now – before you've even written a word?
- How to build your audience and grow your author brand
- Why your book cover design is crucial to making your book a best seller

PURCHASE THE 20-MINUTE AUTHOR BOOK >>> PRE-ORDER NOW!

about the author
MAJA WOLNIK

Maja Wolnik is a passionate book designer, brand strategist and author. Her design agency, Maja Creative, helps entrepreneurs become published authors, by creating beautiful books that help them share their wisdom, leverage their expertise and build a passive income stream.

www.majacreative.com

WHAT I DO

Graphic Design	Book Design	Book Coaching
Brand Strategy	Book Cover Design	Book Marketing
Branding	Book Page Design	Author Branding

stay tuned...

Be the first to know about the book release date, tours, appearances, challenges and giveaways.

| Full Name | Email |
| Type your name | Type your email | JOIN NOW

Join the 20-Minute Author Private Facebook Group to receive FREE book publishing training videos, tips, strategies, plans and more!

JOIN MY FACEBOOK GROUP

OUR 20 DAY CHALLENGE STARTS IN JULY!

STEP 5
start building your fanbase right now

You can start creating a buzz about your book now. It is important to get people intrigued about it. This gives your book life even before it is born into this world.

By promoting your book now, you will start to build a strong fan base while you write. You don't want to spend all this time and energy writing your book only to realise at the end of the process that you have to spend additional months promoting it. No one will know about your book until you tell them about it. Creating brand awareness takes time, so it isessential to use your time wisely and market your book while you write it.

I started telling the story of my book early on, and I began introducing it into my marketing at different stages. There are many ways to do this, but the goal is to create buzz and excitement. The more you talk about your book, the more people will anticipate being able to buy it when it is finally finished.

chapter ten
inspired actions

START PROMOTING YOUR BOOK

I hope this gives you some insight about why it is important to create buzz around your book even before you have finished writing it.

1. Your action for today is to make a list of the different ways you could begin to promote your book now. Think about how you can use the content that you have already written in your book to create some marketing pieces, such as posts on Facebook, LinkedIn, Instagram, Pinterest and your website's landing page or blog.

2. How can you leverage this information? Circle the ideas that appeal to you from the list below:

   Get my book cover designed
   Get a printed sample of my book
   Organise a professional photoshoot
   Start a blog about my book journey
   Create a landing page for my book
   Presell my book
   Do a Kickstarter campaign
   Record a video about my book
   Share excerpts from my book

3. Make a final actionable list of the ones you want to implement.

....
....
....
....
....
....
....
....
....
....
....
....
....

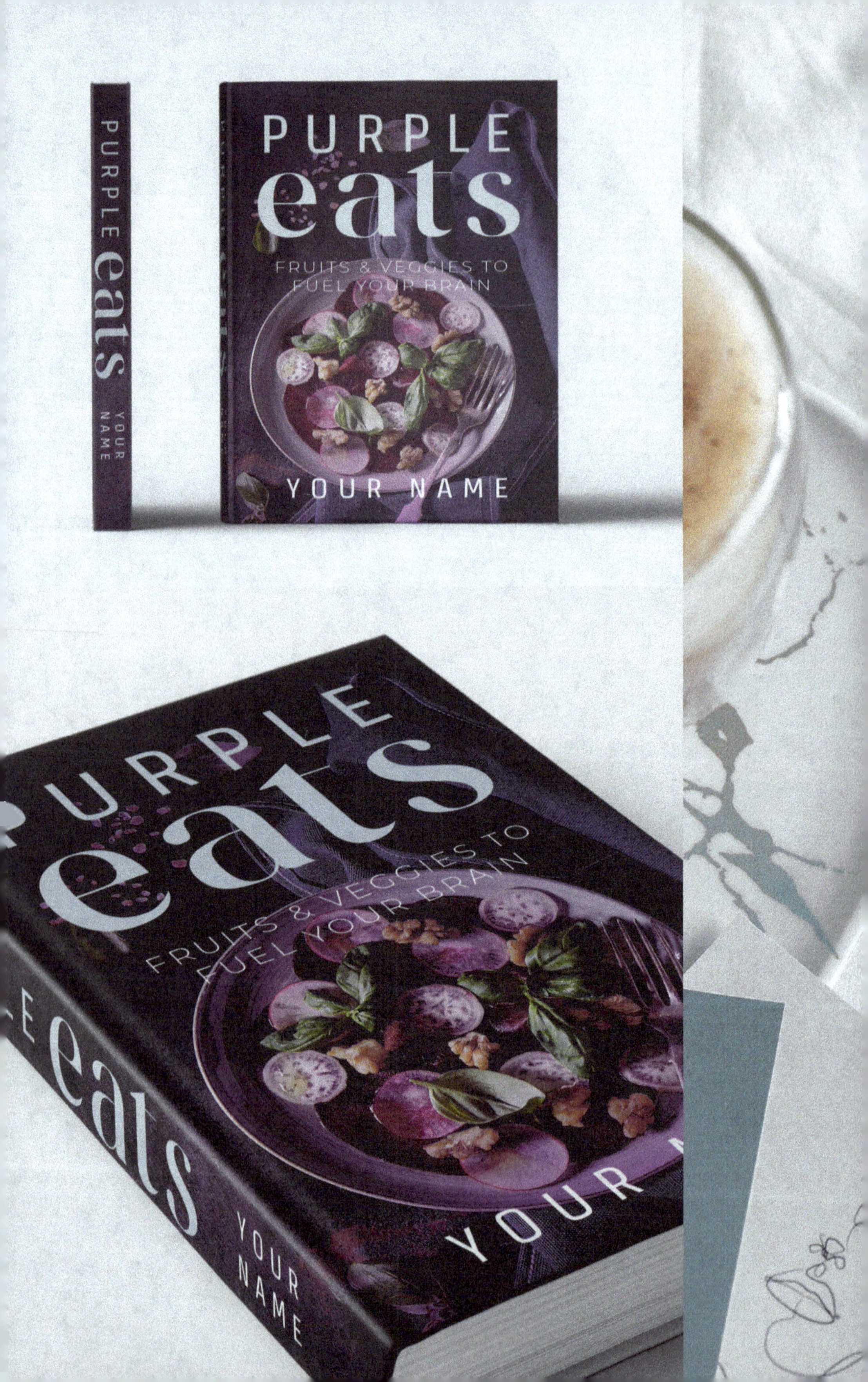
PURPLE eats
YOUR NAME
PURPLE
eats
FRUITS & VEGGIES TO
FUEL YOUR BRAIN
YOUR NAME
URPLE
eats
FRUITS & VEGGIES TO
FUEL YOUR BRAIN
YOUR
eats
YOUR
NAME

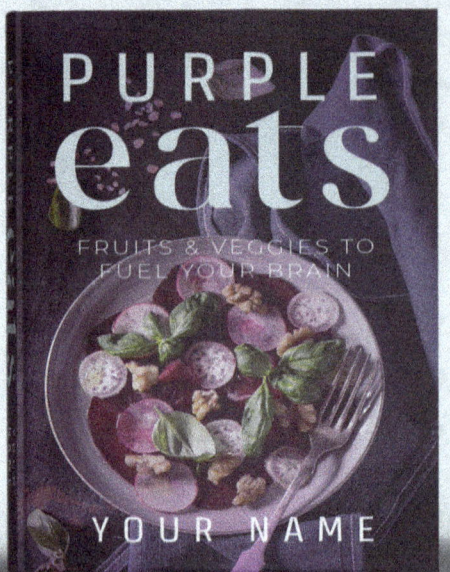

chapter eleven

book covers
THAT CONVERT

When it comes to book cover design, there is an old cliché that says, 'Don't judge a book by its cover'. Fortunately for you, we all judge books by their covers, so you can use this behavior to your advantage.

STEP 1
your book cover is your most important marketing tool

When your reader picks up your book or sees your book online, the first thing they're going to do is judge your book by its cover because they can't read the whole thing on the spot. They can only judge it by the image they're seeing.

The second thing your reader will do is flip your book over and judge it by its back cover by reading your blurb and bio. Your reader has only those two elements to go by when it comes to forming an opinion and making a decision to buy your book.

I believe your book cover is THE most important marketing tool to get your reader to notice, purchase, read, and recommend your book, so your book cover needs to achieve those four goals.

STEP 2
define your book's core idea, message, and feeling

Your book cover needs to capture and convey the essence of your book instantly. What is the core IDEA, MESSAGE, and FEELING that you want to convey to your audience about your book?

Once you decide on this, you will want to design your book cover to convey this experience. This means your book title and subtitle, as well as the fonts, typography, colours, and images that you use all need to tie together to support this single feeling, message, and idea.

STEP 3
your book needs to grab attention

Your book cover needs to grab attention, be memorable, and be easy to see from a distance, whether that's on a bookshelf or in the Google search results. Remember, you will be using this book cover to promote your book over and over again, so you want to make sure that you invest in professional design that will make your book stand out from the crowd.

Just because you are self-publishing your book doesn't mean that your book cover has to look like you've done it yourself in PowerPoint. If you do this, you will come off as an amateur and lose your credibility with your audience. You will be competing against professionally designed book covers, so if you hire a skilled design team to create your cover, you book will be much more likely to succeed.

STEP 4
create a mood board for your book cover

One of the best ways to gain some inspiration for your book cover is to create a Pinterest mood board. Do some research on book covers on Amazon. Start looking up other books in your category. For instance, if you're writing a business book, search for other business books that are similar to yours.

It is important to look at the covers that you will be competing with so that you can figure out how to make your book stand out. Make sure to note which covers are best sellers in their category and use these designs in your cover brainstorming. Find a happy medium between the book covers that appeal to you and those that will appeal to your ideal reader.

> Just because you are self-publishing your book doesn't mean that your book cover has to look like you've done it yourself.

There is a Pinterest add-on for Chrome that allows you to save images to your Pinterest board. Install this extension and start pinning book covers and any other inspiring images to your board.

Ask yourself, what do you like about these covers? Why do you think they are appealing? Which covers don't work for you? Which ones look professional and which ones don't? Make sure to look at the reviews and ratings for these books as well. You want your cover to resemble books that are popular and well-reviewed.

- Take note of the typography—what kind of fonts are used?
- Take note of the imagery—what was the photography or illustration style used?
- Take note of the colour scheme—what mood do you think the colours add to each book?
- Which book covers seem appealing and professional to you?
- Which covers grab your attention?
- What feeling, message, or idea do you get from each cover?

chapter eleven
inspired actions

1) DEFINE YOUR BOOK'S CORE IDEA, MESSAGE, AND FEELING

My core idea for my book cover is:

....
....
....
....
....

My core message for my book cover is:

....
....
....
....
....

My core feeling for my book cover is:

....
....
....
....

2) COLLECT INSPIRATION FOR YOUR BOOK COVER

Start collecting photos, illustrations, and examples of beautiful typography and colours that paint the picture of what you want your book cover to convey.

3) LOOK AT THE COMPETITION

Look up your favourite authors and books—could they yield some inspiration for your own book cover?

....
....
....
....
....
....
....
....
....
....
....
....
....
....
....
....

4) CREATE A PINTEREST MOOD BOARD

Create a Pinterest mood board of book covers and images that inspire you. You don't have to limit yourself to Amazon. You can search any books or images on the internet and save them all to your Pinterest board.

5) SKETCH A MOCKUP BOOK COVER

If you're feeling brave, create a sketch of what you want your book cover to look like. This is a good process to use with your design team to ensure they will get the gist of what you want.

YOUR BOOK INSPIRATION MOOD BOARD

YOUR BOOK COVER SKETCH

WRITTEN BY YOU

Salon Confessions

Memoirs of a Hairdresser

(spine) salon confessions — WRITTEN BY YOU

12

WRITTEN BY YOU

Salon Confessions
Memoirs of a Hairdresser

Salon Confessions

Memoirs of a hairdresser

What is said at the salon, stays at the salon... until now. Award winning hair dresser Jane Smith quickly discovered that her career in hairdressing was more than just about the cut and colour. Each session with a client was like a confessional and over the last three decades in the salon – she's heard it all.

Salon Confessions is a fascinating look at the intimate stories of people from all walks of life. With each hair cut Jane was a witness to peoples most deepest inner thoughts, troubles, secrets and aspirations, which for some reason, they felt comfortable enough to share with their hairdresser. Some are funny, some very tragic and others down right scandalous, but each unique story dives deep into the nitty gritty of life and above all, the strength of the human spirit. A fascinating look behind the scenes of the salon industry, this book ensures you will never look at hair (or your hair dresser) in quite the same way again.

ABOUT THE AUTHOR

Jane Smith is an award winning hair dresser with a career spanning over three decades. She's worked in tiny salons, major chains and boutique establishments for the rich and famous. Salon Confessions is her first book, a memoir, that delves into her personal experiences with her clients, whose actual names are omitted to protect their privacy. Jane is not only a brilliant hair dresser, but also a brilliant listener, and her long term clients have remained on her books not only for gorgeous hair but for the enduring friendship and unique relationship that is formed between patron and hairdresser. You can book an appointment with Jane at www.janesmithhair.com if you want to be featured in her next book.

ISBN 978-1-911223-13-9

chapter twelve

PROVE YOUR AUTHOR
credibility

After your front cover has done its job and your reader has picked up your book, the next thing your potential buyer will do is flip your book over and read the back cover. Your back cover is your opportunity to prove your credibility as an expert in your field, which converts your casual reader into a definite buyer.

Professional layout and copywriting are crucial for establishing your credibility. You have only a couple of seconds to grab attention and entice your reader to buy your book. When a potential buyer is glancing at the back cover of your book, you want them to quickly and easily understand your expertise as an author. If the layout looks long and boring, your potential buyer may put your book back on the shelf.

STEP 1
commission a professional blurb and author bio

Your book blurb and author bio need to sell your book. When writing your author bio, go back to your 'why statement' from Chapter 3 and ask yourself why you have written this book? What makes you the expert or authority on this topic? What experience or knowledge can you share about yourself that will give you credibility?

When writing your book blurb, you've only got a couple of seconds to convey what your book is about. Go back to Chapter 4 and review your ideal reader profile. Get into their hearts and minds and think about the kinds of challenges they are having. How does your book solve those challenges? What exactly do your readers get from reading your book?

This concise paragraph will be used across multiple platforms to sell your book online, not just on your back cover, so it is essential to get it right. In general, only the first few words of your blurb are featured online, so you need a strong hook to capture attention and entice someone to continue reading what they're about to click on. We have professional copywriters on my team that can help you craft this copy to make sure that it sells and converts.

It all starts with your book cover.

Salon Confessions
Memoirs of a hairdresser

What is said at the salon, stays at the salon... until now. Award winning hair dresser Jane Smith quickly discovered that her career in hairdressing was more than just about the cut and colour. Each session with a client was like a confessional and over the last three decades in the salon – she's heard it all.

Salon Confessions is a fascinating look at the intimate stories of people from all walks of life. With each hair cut Jane was a witness to peoples most deepest inner thoughts, troubles, secrets and aspirations, which for some reason, they felt comfortable enough to share with their hairdresser. Some are funny, some very tragic and others down right scandalous, but each unique story dives deep into the nitty gritty of life and above all, the strength of the human spirit. A fascinating look behind the scenes of the salon industry, this book ensures you will never look at hair (or your hairdresser) in quite the same way again.

ABOUT THE AUTHOR

Jane Smith is an award winning hair dresser with a career spanning over three decades. She's worked in tiny salons, major chains and boutique establishments for the rich and famous. Salon Confessions is her first book, a memoir, that delves into her personal experiences with her clients, whose actual names are omitted to protect their privacy. Jane is not only a brilliant hair dresser, but also a brilliant listener, and her long term clients have remained on her books not only for gorgeous hair but for the enduring friendship and unique relationship that is formed between patron and hairdresser. You can book an appointment with Jane at www.janesmithhair.com if you want to be featured in her next book.

ISBN 978-1-911223-13-9

STEP 2
commission a professionally designed cover

As mentioned in Chapter 11, your book cover is THE most important marketing tool when it comes to promoting your book. My advice is to get your book cover designed as early as possible so you can start promoting your book NOW. The fact is that you don't have to finish writing your manuscript before you can start promoting your book.

When you have your book cover designed with your professionally written author bio and book blurb, you can start sharing images of your book on social media. You can use your blurb and bio to create a press release to pitch your book for arranging interviews on podcasts. You can also use this information to write a landing page to collect emails and pre-sale orders of your book. Getting people excited about your book before it is published will give you the motivation to finish it faster, and it all starts with your book cover.

You don't have to finish writing your manuscript before you can start promoting your book.

chapter twelve
inspired actions

PROVE YOUR AUTHOR CREDIBILITY

1. List at least three reasons that give you credibility or make you an expert in the topic you are discussing in your book.

2. Think about at least three solutions your book provides to your ideal readers.

....
....
....
....
....
....
....
....
....
....
....
....
....
....
....
....
....
....
....

3. Get your book cover professionally designed and your author bio and book blurb professionally written.

13

LUXURIOUS APARTMENTS

How to make small spaces luxe

WRITTEN BY YOU

chapter thirteen

PAGE TURNING
design

While the front cover and back cover are crucial to grabbing attention and getting your book into the hands of your readers, beautiful interior page design tells your story and keeps your readers engaged.

STEP 1
clarify your book design

I want you to consider the interior pages of your book. Are you writing a book that is text heavy and needs a simple, professional layout? Or are you wanting something more? Are you working on a book that needs an intricate design with beautiful chapter separations? Are you writing a coffee table or magazine style book that needs a custom designed layout with charts, infographics, and glossy pictures? Are you developing a comprehensive workbook for your programs and courses that includes sections for your audience to fill out?

A book isn't just words on a page—take time today to give this careful consideration. You want your book to be engaging, and you want your readers to have an immersive experience when reading your book. The words you write do paint a picture, but there are so many creative ways that you can bring a book to life. With beautiful imagery, art direction, layout, and design, you can communicate complex information and help tell the story.

Have a think about the interior pages of your book and start researching some examples of book layouts that you love. Again, you can do this on Pinterest, but also consider picking up some books around your house and take note of the formatting. What do the chapter headings look like? Are there intro pages that stand out? Is there a system to the book, or does each page look different?

No two books are the same, so consider what type of book design your manuscript pages will fall into.

STEP 2
consider a simple book design

If you're writing a text-based novel, memoir, or business book, your page layout can be typeset simply with black and white text and no images or special text treatments. Just because a design is simple, doesn't mean it can't also be beautiful. Our design team can help you create an effective layout using elements such as typography, paragraph styles, chapter openings, and engaging chapter titles that will give your audience an enjoyable reading experience. This format is also adjustable for ebooks on the Kindle or iPad platforms, where elements will flow freely depending on the type of device the book is being viewed from.

YOUR HOME IS IMPORTANT

· IT STARTED WITH A PLAN ·

Lorem ipsum dolor sit amet, consectetur adipiscing elit. Nulla laoreet risus vitae mattis euismod. Praesent fusce sodales sapien felis ultrices, eget fermentum diam eget laoreet. Nulla consequat turpis ornare, vitae blandit felis placerat. Pellentesque mauris Pellentesque elementum turpis aliquet. Orci ligula posuere vitae tempus turpis placerat. Quisque a tellus vel lacus mattis dapibus primis in faucibus. Nullam ac Purus eget tortor feugiat dictum, malesuada fames ac ante ipsum primis in faucibus.

WE SHAPE OUR HOMES AND THEN OUR HOMES SHAPE US.

· WINSTON CHURCHILL ·

Integer ac Aenean convallis nec mi vehicula tincidunt. Donec quis odio ac lectus blandit fringilla et vel nunc. Nam in risus tincidunt felis consequat laoreet. Aliquam vitae tincidunt tortor. Ut velit ipsum, cursus a imperdiet quis, facilisis vitae nisi. Maecenas ullamcorper orci eget mi tincidunt scelerisque. Quisque malesuada ligula vel nisl porttitor, varius pulvinar dui hendrerit. Donec maximus nibh in sapien lacinia, non ultricies velit iaculis. Fusce at purus eu nunc pla cerat tempor quis ut metus. Aliquam gravida arcu id mauris bla ndit, in tincidunt lacus volutpat. Interdum otenjvn etes male suada fames ac ante ipsum primis in faucibus. Donec mattis, dolor nec congue rutrum, arcu lectus vehicula enim, non auctor magna risus sed velit. Fusce fermentum sapien sodales mauris bibendum, eget condimentum diam posuere. Quisque posuere est sed nulla pulvinar, sit amet consectetur ex facilisis. Orci varius natoque penatibus et magnis dis parturient montes, nascetur ridiculus mus. Integer non porttitor leo. Vivamus sit amet pharetra massa. Vestibulum at tristique diam. Cras sed elit eu lorem posuere vulputate. Pellentesque at

> "THE DETAILS ARE NOT THE DETAILS. THEY MAKE THE DESIGN."

sapien gravida, auctor mi sit amet, condimentum augue. In eu ipsum neque. Vivamus lectus ex, porta eget nulla nec, dictum faucibus purus. Etiam congue semper elit. Donec non volutpat massa. Aenean quam lacus, molestie in aliquam in, tempor non lacus. Praesent cursus nec orci ut aliquet. Class aptent taciti sociosqu ad litora torquent per conubia nostra, per inceptos himenaeos. Vivamus ultrices felis sit amet commodo hendrerit. Ut pulvinar maximus felis, vel lobortis sem finibus id. In mattis rutrum laoreet. Morbi augue nisi, ultrices et risus feugiat, pretium faucibus tortor.

1. Sed auctor lorem nec quam congue gravida. Praesent a condimentum elit. Aenean dapibus
2. nisi eget ex varius eleifend. In facilisis urna felis, eu semper turpis semper vitae. Orci varius natoque penatibus et magnis dis
3. parturient montes, nascetur ridiculus mus. Praesent turpis ex, aliquet eget placerat s
4. conean justo ex, dapibus interdum bibendum eget, tempor non mauris. Cras in accunsectetu
5. r a nulla. Proin sapien neque, consequat eget dolor in, feugiat tincidunt nisl. Vestibulum dictum nisi massa, sit amet interdum lorem feugiat a.

Nullam euismod consectetur turpis semper finibus. Integer dapibus commodo nibh, non cursus leo interdum et. Aemsan libero, vitae elementum massa. Mauris eu commodo odio, id vestibulum erat. In at justo quis libero vehicula

STEP 3
consider a complex book design

If you want your interior pages to be more interesting, consider a complex page layout with text, images, and illustrations in full colour. This type of book design is ideal for more creative business books, biographies and memoirs, self-help books, art and photography books, coffee table books, cook books and any other books that require special text treatments, colour images, and creative design elements. With this format, the layout is an important element that enhances the reading experience and adds to the manuscript. Our design team can create a unique visual language and a repeatable system for your interior pages that will help you elegantly communicate the ideas in your text and make your book a delight to read and flip through. A complex book design can also double as a downloadable ebook in PDF format, where the elements will remain static on the page, but you can add interactive embellishments.

You want your book to be engaging, and you want your readers to have an immersive experience when reading your book.

STEP 4
consider a custom book design

A custom design is perfect if your book requires special attention to each spread. This is ideal for custom designed books, such as manuals, workbooks, journals, technical books, corporate histories, children's books, and creative business books where every page is unique and requires distinct text treatments, full colour images and illustrations, and creative design elements that change throughout the book. With this format, the design is as crucial to the success of the book as the manuscript is and the audience is seeking something rare and highly creative. Our design team can bring every single page of your book to life with carefully crafted art direction, typography treatments, custom illustration, professional photography, icons, charts and graphic elements. With a custom book design, the sky is the limit when it comes to creative expression.

> the design is as crucial to the success of the book as is the manuscript and the audience is seeking something rare and highly creative.

STEP 5
contact us for your book mapping session

The design process takes time, so I really want you to start thinking about your interior page design early on. You want to be ready to share your inspiration and ideas with your design team so they can start designing the look and feel of your book while you're still writing your manuscript.

That process can happen simultaneously, and your book can be rolled out and finalised once your manuscript is finished and final edits have been made. That's exactly what we do at Maja Creative—we start the interior page design process early while you're still working on your book.

Not sure which what type of book design will be most suitable for your type of book? You can book in for your Book Mapping Session (https://bit.ly/BookMappingSession). In our meeting, we will discuss your book in depth and cover some of the creative and strategic ways that we can bring your book cover and interior design to life.

The layout design is an important element that enhances the reading experience.

YOUR HOME IS IMPORTANT

- IT STARTED WITH A PLAN -

Lorem ipsum dolor sit amet, consectetur adipiscing elit. Nulla laoreet risus vitae mattis cursus mod. Praesent Fusce Sodales sapien vitae magna fermentum, eget blandit felis ultrices. Nulla consequat diam eget aliquam placerat. Nullam aliquet turpis ornare, ultricies enim eget, lacinia mauris. Pellentesque elementum lacus sit amet ligula posuere, vitae tempus turpis aliquet. Quisque at tellus vel lacus mattis dapibus. Interdum et malesuada fames ac ante ipsum primis in faucibus. Nullam ac purus eget tortor feugiat dictum.

WE SHAPE
OUR HOMES
AND THEN
OUR HOMES
SHAPE US.

- WINSTON CHURCHILL -

---

1. PLAN YOUR LAYOUT

Erere euismod vlorewadiusgao e nec lacodubus. Re lentesque ac sapien gravida, auctor mi sit amet dimentum augue. In eu ipsum neque. Vivamus lus ex, porta eget nulla nec. dictum nostra ut.

2. THINK ABOUT YOUR NEEDS

Etiam congue semper elit. Dedhkones, non volutae massa. Aenean quam lacus, samolestie, in aliquam in, tempor non lacus. Maecenas enim ullamcorper ad orci ut aliquet. Class aptent taciti sociosqu litora torquent per conubia nostra, per inceptos himenaeos.

1. HOW BIG IS YOUR FAMILY

Nec quam congue gravida, Praesent, astdib condimentum elit. Aenean dapibus nisl, eget Morbi augue nisl, ultrices et ris varius eleifend.

2. HOW MUCH ROOM DO YOU NEED

Infacilisi Vivamus ultrices urnafelis, euismpo turpis semper felis sit a pret nunt faucibus. vitae Orci varius natoque penatibus et magnis m

3. ADD RELAXATION SPACE

Parturient montes, nascetur ridiculus mus. Praesmet commodo hendrerit pla cerat

---

Teger ac aenean convallis, nec mi vehicula tincidunt. Donec quis odio ac lectus unt felis consequat laoreet. Aliquam Ut tortor veliasserter ipsu amet hc cdcduc sis amet imperdiet quis, dvid-facilisis vitaelum nisl. Maece nas ullamcorper orci eget mi tincidunt scelerisque ligu Quisque malesuada La vel nisl portitor varius nec maximus nibh in sapien lacinia, non ultricies velit pla cerat tempor bus nunc, Fusce at purus eu arcu id mauris bla ndit. In tincidunt lacus volutpat. In terdum oterjvm etes male

Donec fames ac ante ipsum primis in faucibus. Donec mattis, dolor non vehicula rutrum, arcu lectus vestibula erim, non auctor magna suada sus sed velit. Fusce fermen tum sapien sodales mayris

" THE DETAILS ARE
NOT THE DETAILS.
THEY MAKE THE
DESIGN. "

ex facilisis, consquedamero dimentum dicatam posuere Quinesque posuere esssed sectetur ex, facilisit. Orci variusnatoque penatibus et magnis dis parturient montes. Integer non amet Vivamus sit amet pharetra. Vestibulum at tri cofvcortfoque diam Crasse sed eli loret eu lorem po sus natoque penatibus et.

chapter thirteen
inspired actions

MAP OUT YOUR BOOK DESIGN

1. Create a mood board and gather design inspiration for your book's interior page layout.

List three book titles whose book interior pages inspire you:

....
....
....
....

DESIGN NOTES

....
....
....
....
....
....
....
....
....
....

YOUR MOOD BOARD

2. Determine what type of book design would be best suitable for your book

My interior book design will be:
- ☐ Simple Book Design
- ☐ Complex Book Design
- ☐ Custom Book Design

DESIGN NOTES

....
....
....
....
....
....
....
....
....
....
....
....
....
....

3. Book in for your Book Mapping Session with Maja Creative. (https://bit.ly/BookMappingSession).

PSYCHOLOGY OF SUCCESS

MINDSET IS key

YOUR NAME HERE

14

chapter fourteen

YOUR BOOK QUESTIONS
answered

If you're doing the 20 minute Author 20 Day Challenge then today is Q&A Thursday… or Monday, or Tuesday or Wednesday or perhaps Friday! Whatever day of the week it may be, this is the day we answer any questions about book design, book publishing or author branding that our clients and participants send in.

STEP 1
make a list of your questions

As you go through the journey of becoming a published author, you might have some questions that come up that are not immediately addressed in this book.

I've saved this section of the book specifically for that – here you can start making a list of any questions that might pop up. There is no such thing as a silly question! I am here to help you become a published author, so ask away.

STEP 2
submit your questions

Once you've got a few questions that you think need answering, submit them by posting a comment in the 20-minute Author Facebook Group, sending them directly to me via messenger or by commenting on the Q&A video in the 20-minute Author Challenge.

STEP 3
review previous q&a sessions

If you're doing the 20-minute Author Challenge, make sure you review any previous Q&A Session replays from our video library – your question might already be answered in there! If not, we will do our best to include your question in our next Q&A Session.

chapter 14
inspired actions

MAKE A LIST OF ALL YOUR QUESTIONS

1. Make list of any questions you might have in relation to book publishing, book design and author branding.

....

....

....

....

....

....

....

....

....

....

2. Submit your questions via messenger, as a comment or directly in the 20-minute Author 20 Day Challenge.

3. Review any previous Q&A Sessions in our video library to check if your question has been answered.

15

AUTHOR NAME
Pull A Card
EVERYDAY TAROT FOR A LIFE
FILLED WITH MAGIC

AUTHOR NAME
Pull A Card
EVERYDAY TAROT FOR A LIFE
FILLED WITH MAGIC

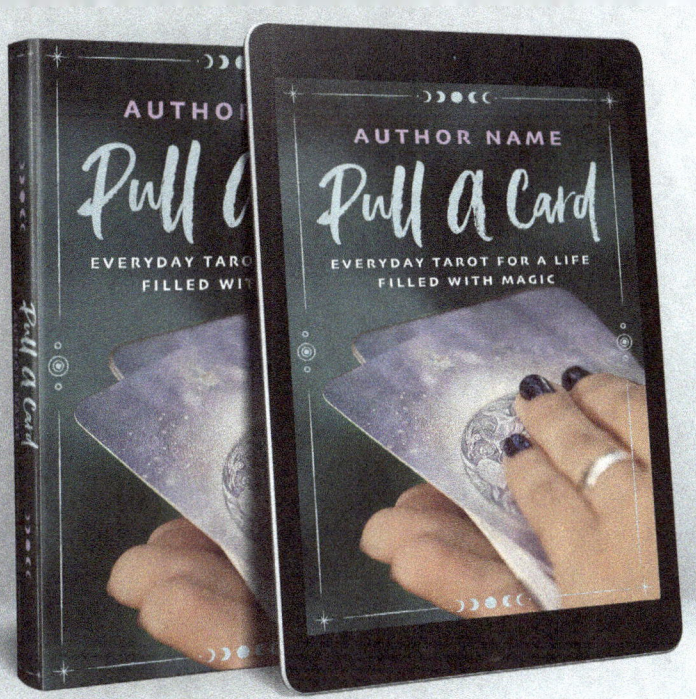

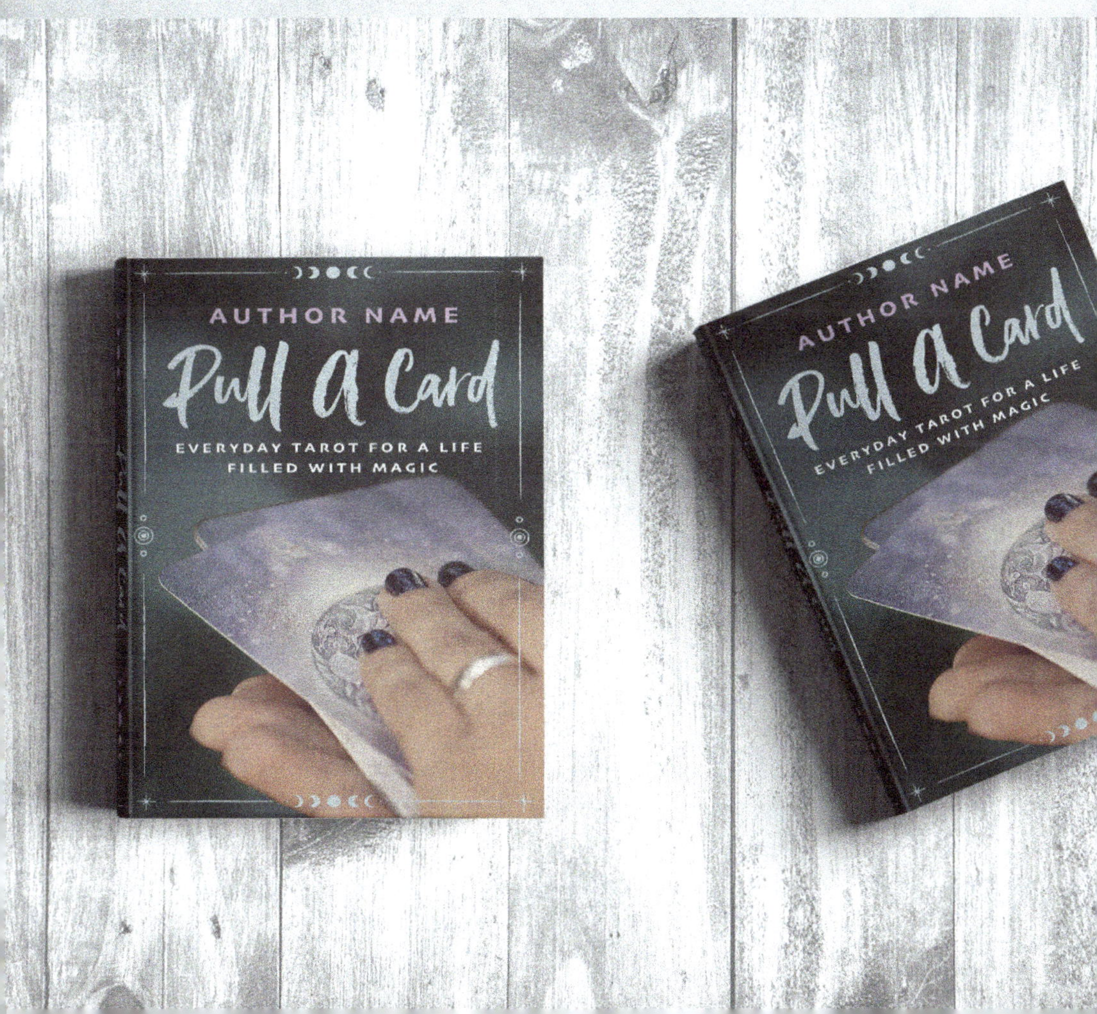

chapter fifteen

book editing
FUNDAMENTALS

'Do I need an editor?' is a question that I frequently get asked, often followed by 'Can't I just write my own book and edit it myself and then get it published?' The simple truth is that yes, of course you can... but would you really want to? Today I want to dive deep into the book editing process and share some simple tips with you to get the best manuscript back from your editor.

STEP 1
hire a professional editor

If you've been following this book, you must realise by now that you should leave it up to us, the professionals, to design your book cover and the interior pages of your book. You could do it yourself—using Microsoft Paint, for example—but we both know this would not give you a professional result.

The same goes for your manuscript! You could edit your book yourself, or get a friend, cousin or a well-meaning volunteer to do it, but you run the risk of showing your audience something that looks as if it has been slapped together.

If you want your book to be a professional statement for you and your business, you need a professional editor to review and correct your manuscript. An editor is going to be able to take your words and ideas, and present you as your best self. This will allow your book to serve as an effective conduit for your business, encouraging your ideal reader to engage with you in more impactful ways.

> *An editor is going to be able to take your words, your ideas, and present you as your best self.*

You might be an expert in the topic that you're writing your book about, but that doesn't necessarily make you an amazing writer. None of us were born with author skills, so a professional editor will make your manuscript polished and professional.

STEP 2
consider the type of edit you will require

When I first started working with my editor, Caitlin Freeman, I had no idea that there were multiple ways that a manuscript can be edited.

Depending on your writing skills and the quality of your manuscript, you may need the following types of edits to your manuscript.

Copy Edit

When people talk about editing, they are often thinking of copy editing. In copy editing, an editor reviews and corrects your book's grammar, punctuation, spelling, and other basic mechanics of language. The copy edit usually comes in at the very end of an edit.

Substantive Edit

In a substantive edit, the editor reviews and improves the content, style, and format of your manuscript. Your editor will not just be playing comma police. They will review the overall structure of your book, and they are likely to move paragraphs and chapters around. Are you expressing the ideas that you want to convey? Is your writing clear and concise? Are your format and layout consistent? An editor will shape your rough draft into a manuscript that will communicate most clearly with your ideal reader.

Manuscript Critique

A manuscript critique is an editor's review. You are asking your editor, 'Give me your overall opinions and impressions'. Your editor will give you an examination of your writing style and ways to enhance it, specific advice on how to improve the narrative to keep your readers engaged, and feedback on where you're missing opportunities to develop your story.

STEP 3
let go and trust

Step away from your manuscript. Having just been through the editing process myself, that is my best advice to you. When you are writing your book, you are too close to it to be objective. You might feel tempted to start editing your book when you're still writing it. You might decide to write a chapter and then start editing it immediately afterwards—don't. It's much better to get everything out of your head first.

When I wrote this book, I used voice-to-text, transcribed everything, and then added elements by typing. Afterwards, I made the mistake of printing out my manuscript and trying to look at it with fresh eyes, but I got stuck in this process. I wound up wasting about a week and a half trying to edit something that I was too fatigued to read clearly. If you've finished your first draft, your job is done! Step away from the manuscript and send it off to your editor immediately.

Your editor will be able to see your manuscript as your ideal reader will experience it.

Trust your editor. You will be amazed at the quality of work that comes back to you. There will be a bit of back and forth, but it is your editor's job to see the big picture and help you realise your vision.

> Your editor will not just be playing comma police here, they will review the overall structure of your book.

chapter fifteen
inspired actions

1) HIRE AN EDITOR

If you want your book to connect with your audience don't edit your own book. Invest in professional services that will make your manuscript shine.

Contact details for my editor are:

Name:
....

Email:
....

Phone Number:
....

2) CONSIDER WHAT TYPE OF EDIT YOU WILL NEED

I require a:

☐ Copy Edit

☐ Substantial Edit / Line Edit

☐ Manuscript Critique

3) STEP AWAY FROM YOUR MANUSCRIPT

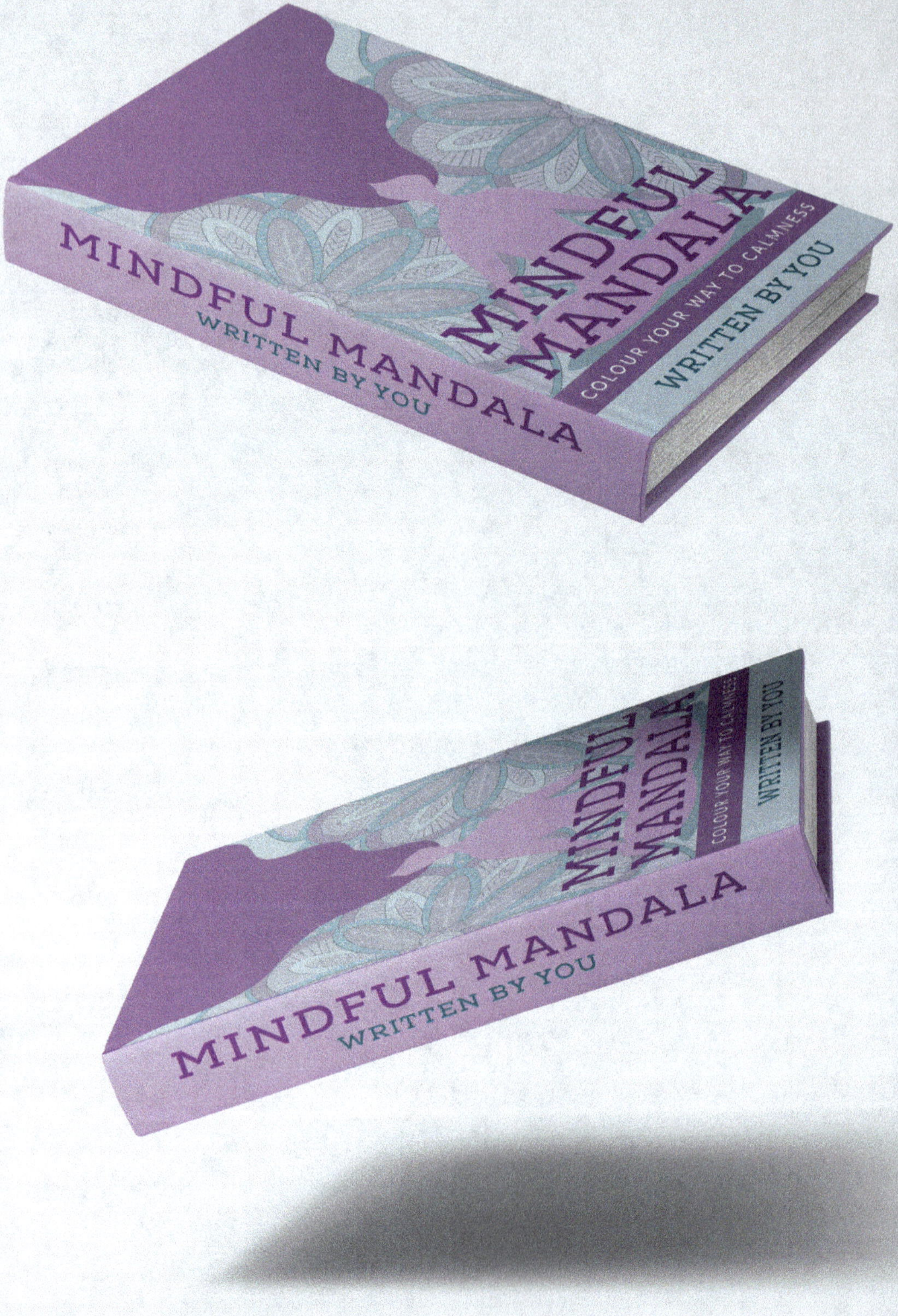
MINDFUL MANDALA
COLOUR YOUR WAY TO CALMNESS
WRITTEN BY YOU
MINDFUL MANDALA
WRITTEN BY YOU
MINDFUL MANDALA
COLOUR YOUR WAY TO CALMNESS
WRITTEN BY YOU
MINDFUL MANDALA
WRITTEN BY YOU

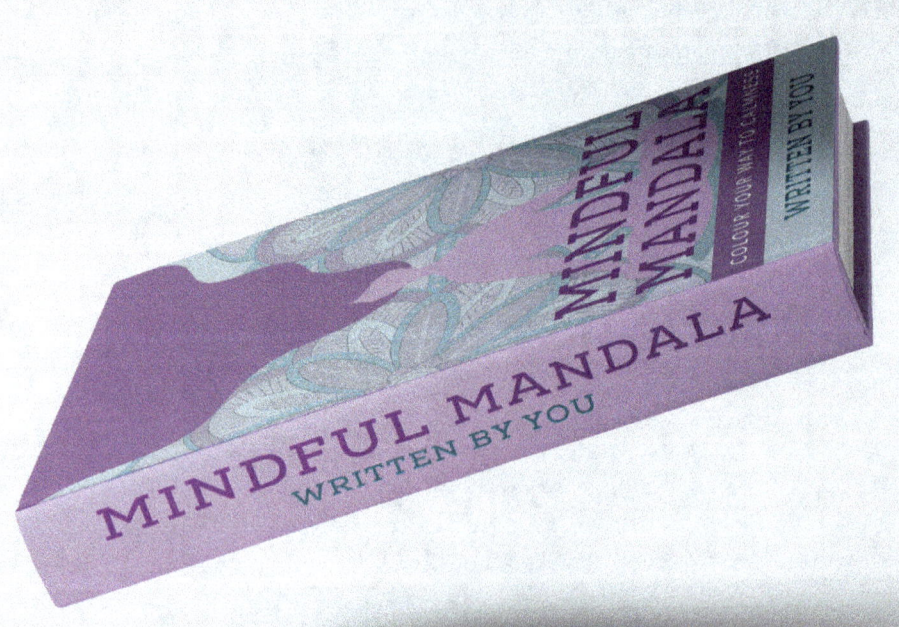

16

chapter sixteen

HOW TO GET OUT OF
a book rut

At some point in your book journey, you are going to get stuck and feel like you're not getting anywhere with your writing. I found that this usually happens around day seven if you're doing the 20-Day Challenge or towards the end. Often when you're at the last 25 percent of your book, your attention wanes, and your writing comes to a bit of a halt.

STEP 1
change locations within your house

One way to stay motivated is to change locations when you are working on your book. If you find that you spend a lot of time in one particular spot when working on your book, whether it's at your desk, your office, your bedroom, or any other spot, I want you to switch it up and change location.

Right now, at the time of writing this book, we are in the midst of a global pandemic because of Covid-19, so there are a lot of restrictions, and we are all advised to stay home. If you can't get outside, it could mean that you need to go into another room or try a different area in the house other than your usual location.

Changing up your environment can help creativity.

The first time I did the 20-Day Challenge and was feeling stuck with my book, it was a gorgeous day in Melbourne, so I decided to move out onto my balcony and work in the sunshine.

Changing up your environment can help creativity. It's also a good idea to avoid using spots where you normally work, sleep, or relax so you don't get distracted from writing by your normal routines. I like working on my book at my kitchen table or the couch instead of in my home office so that it feels different and I am not tempted to do other types of work when I want to be writing.

STEP 2
get a change of scenery

You could also try going to your local cafe or library to work on your book or get out of town completely. A good way to get some fast results with your book is to go away somewhere nice for a few days and do an intensive writing sprint.

One of my clients who is a business coach rented a house by himself and wrote 40,000 words in only three days! Why? Because he had been writing the book in his head for decades; he just needed the time and space to focus and get it all out.

Many years ago, when I was living in Vancouver, Canada, I travelled to an artist colony in Costa Rica and met writers and authors there who were dedicating a whole month to write and finish their books. It was a beautiful, quiet location in the middle of a jungle, with limited Wi-Fi.

Another client of mine is a psychologist who rented out a stunning beach house along the Great Ocean Road to write her book. This unique house sits on a pole, overlooking the ocean. I've posted a picture of it in the 20-Minute Author Group. She had always dreamed of owning a beach house, so this house was inspiration for her to write her book and infuse that intention into her book for doubled success.

STEP 3
recharge in nature

If your brain has turned to mush, it can be helpful to stop everything and get out in nature. Head out into the forest or dip your toes in the sand. Going out in the fresh air can help get new ideas flowing and get more oxygen into your brain.

It's important to take a break and get a new perspective. Doing these activities will boost your creativity and help you start to think differently. If you change location, you will be able to minimise distractions and dedicate your focus to your book.

STEP 4
hire a book coach or ghostwriter

If writing your book is proving to be challenging for you, and life and business keep getting in the way of you making progress, consider hiring a book coach or a ghostwriter to help you finally finish your book. A book coach is someone that will guide you through the whole process.

They will be like your book cheerleader, giving you structure and accountability to get your book done.

A ghostwriter is a professional writer that you can hire to write your book for you. They conduct interviews with you and gather all the information necessary to write your book for you using your words and ideas. Ghostwriters use your content, your ideas, and your current manuscript (if you've started). Think of them like a collaborative writing partner that turns your spoken words into a book that is ready to be designed and published.

The benefits of working with either a book coach or a ghostwriter is that you will get your book done much faster than if you tried to do it by yourself. I want you to consider that while you are an expert in your book's field or topic, and you have an amazing story to share, you may wish to seek out professional expertise when it comes to writing your book, especially if this is your first book. At Maja Creative, we're committed to helping our clients get their books done fast, so our team includes professional ghostwriters and book coaches that help guide our clients through all the steps.

chapter sixteen
inspired actions

1) KEEP MOVING FORWARD WITH YOUR BOOK

Find the best solution for you if you're stuck in a rut. If you're not stuck, keep going, but come back to this chapter if you hit a brick wall. Even if you are not stuck, you can explore some of these actionable options:

1. Change your location. What's your dream location? Where would you love to get away to work on your book? How can you make it happen?

   ....
   ....

2. The perfect location for me to work on my book is

   ....
   ....

3. Accommodation options I've found are

   ....
   ....

4. What I need to make this happen is

   ....
   ....

2) GET OUT OF TOWN AND DO AN INTENSIVE WRITING SPRINT.

3) HIRE A BOOK COACH OR A GHOSTWRITER.

Do you need a book coach or a ghostwriter?
Rate yourself on a scale of 1 – 10 below.

Writing my book comes naturally to me:

Not at all — — *Yes, it's flowing*

1   2   3   4   5   6   7   8   9   10

I'm getting traction with my book and meeting my goals:

I've hardly started — I'm halfway through — I'm nearly finished

1   2   3   4   5   6   7   8   9   10

How long have you been working on your book?

Over 12 months   — 6-12 months —   1-6 months

1   2   3   4   5   6   7   8   9   10

If you scored below 5 on any of the above, consider hiring a book coach or a ghostwriter to help you write your book.

MINDFUL MANDALA
COLOUR YOUR WAY TO CALMNESS
WRITTEN BY YOU

MINDFUL MANDALA
COLOUR YOUR WAY TO CALMNESS
WRITTEN BY YOU

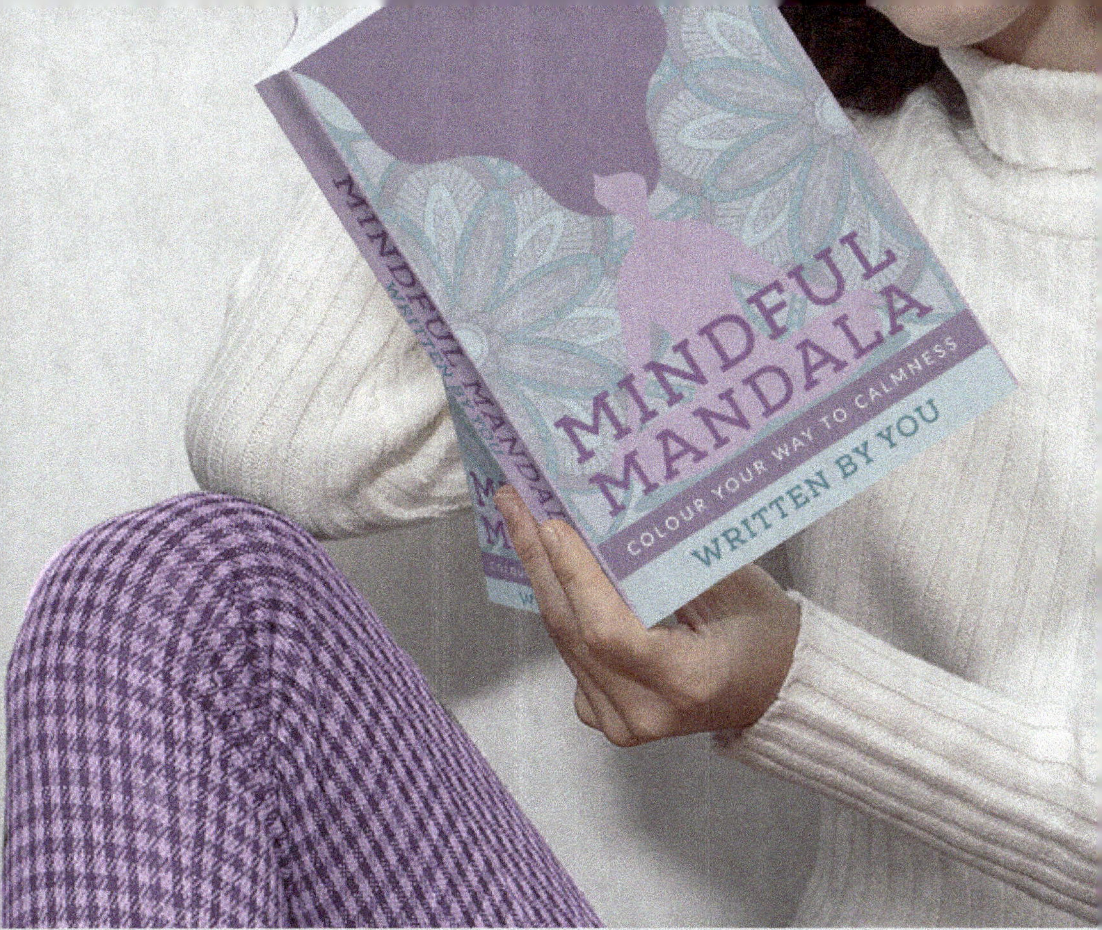

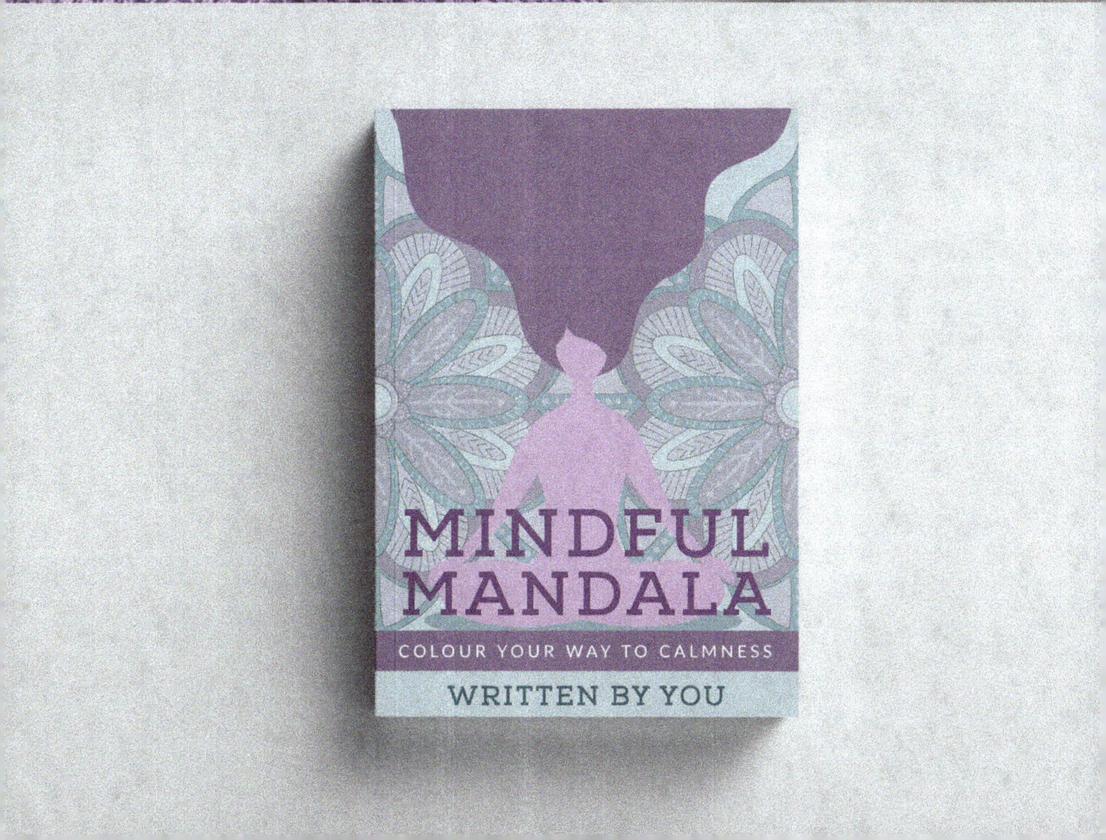

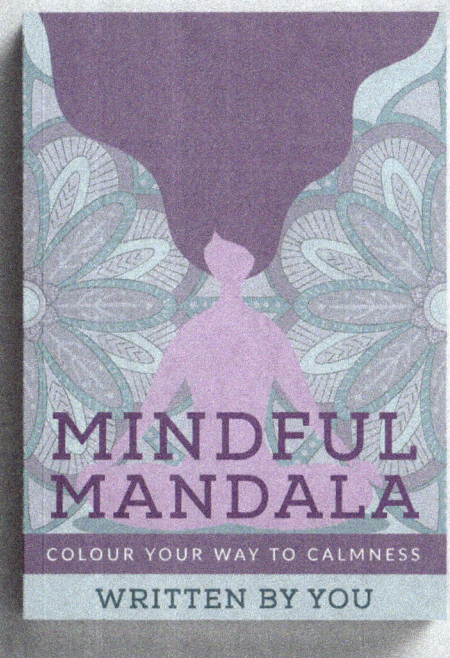

17

WE ARE ALL MADE OF
stardust
a simple guide to astrology
WRITTEN BY YOU
stardust
WRITTEN BY YOU

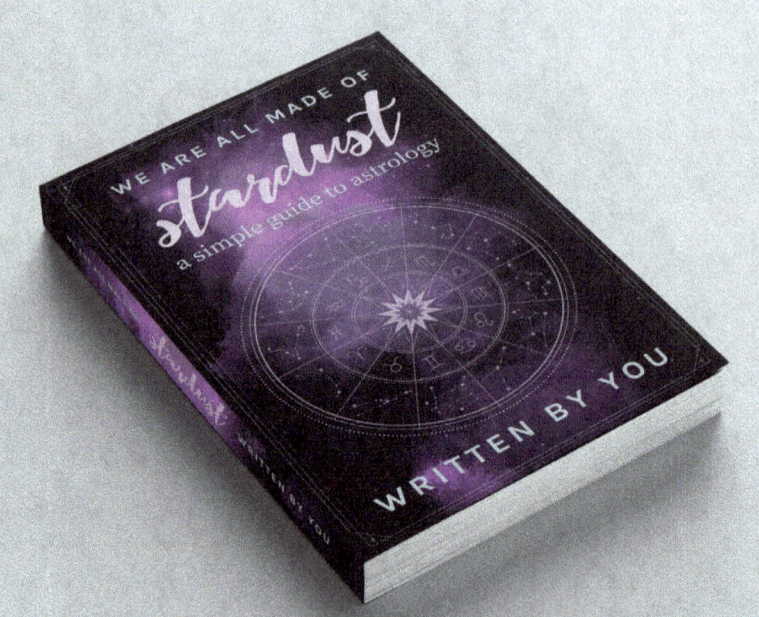

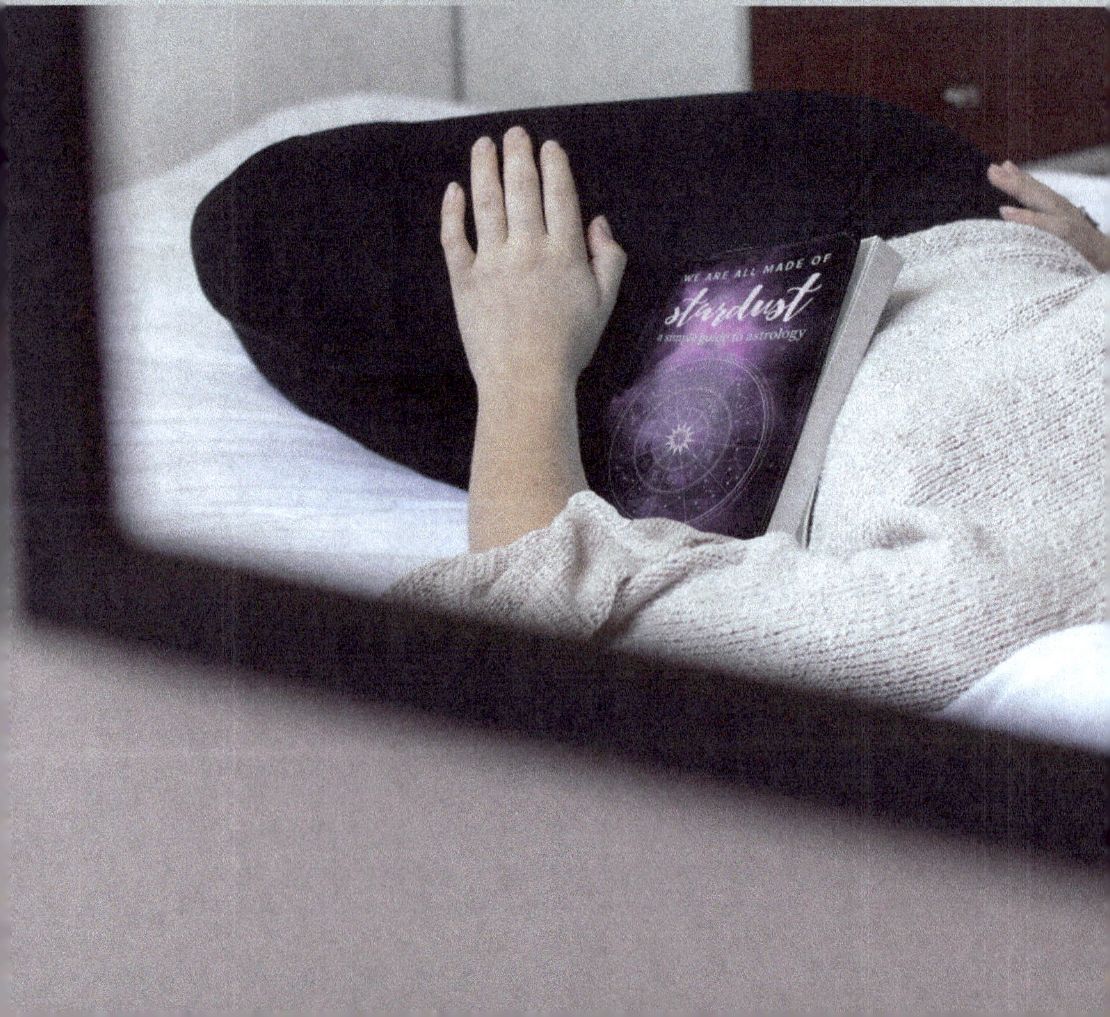
WE ARE ALL MADE OF
stardust
a simple guide to astrology

chapter seventeen

AUTHOR
branding

When it comes to marketing your book, there is one thing that is more important than your book cover and your book itself, and that is your author branding. Establishing your author brand can help you attract the right audience, allowing you to successfully market your book and boost your sales. Your author brand will raise your credibility in your field and help open many doors, especially if you want to make a bigger impact and become a speaker or influencer.

create your personal brand

When I talk about author branding, I mean the perception that people have of you as an author in the marketplace. In the world that we live in today, people buy brands, not just books, so it is important to build a credible author brand. Your brand allows people to recognise you, like you, trust you, buy from you, and eventually become raving fans of your book and your work. Your author brand could be the difference between the success and failure of your book, no matter how well your book is written.

If you're a first-time author, chances are that no one has heard of you, so it is important to start creating and building your brand, your platform, and your audience as early as possible in the piece.

Here are four points I want you to consider when building your author brand.

STEP 1
establish your brand values

A brand is a person's gut feeling about a product, service or company. As an author, you are the brand, and whether you like it or not, your author brand will be judged by how others perceive it and experience it. You can help influence this by actively deciding how you present yourself to your readers. You need to ask yourself, what do you stand for as an author? Your brand values are the foundation of your author brand. This is your belief system and the key messages that need to be reflected in your brand. As humans, we connect best when we share the same values. Your brand values generally stem from your personal values, so consider the core values that you want to resonate with your audience.

> *As humans, we connect best when we share the same values.*

Your author brand could be the difference between the success and failure of your book, no matter how well your book is written.

THE HERO

THE LOVER

THE SAGE

THE OUTLAW

THE CREATOR

THE REGULAR GUY/GIRL

THE INNOCENT

THE EXPLORER

THE MAGICIAN

THE JESTER

THE CAREGIVER

THE RULER

STEP 2
consider your brand personality

How would you describe your personality in a few words? As an author, your author brand is really your personal brand. While there may be multiple sides to your persona, when it comes to marketing your book and author brand, decide which aspects you'd like to share with the world at large. Successful brands have a strong sense of identity, one that mirrors the hopes and aspirations of their customers. Your audience is looking to connect with you, so be authentic, yet see yourself as a leader—they're looking to you and your book for something they lack. Establishing your brand personality will help you find your unique 'voice' and determine how your brand will translate visually in your marketing—fonts, colours, and imagery.

At Maja Creative, we work with Brand Archetypes to help you develop your brand personality. Developed by psychologists Carl Jung and Joseph Campbell, there are twelve archetypes that create a persona. The concept of archetypes is aligned with neuroscience research showing that people make intuitive decisions and are driven by unconscious emotional goals. These archetypes can be easily understood because they evoke deep emotions that we all identify with. Using brand archetypes such as the Hero, the Creator, the Outlaw, the Magician, etc. provides a framework for your brand's personality and makes it easier to tell your brand story. If you would like to know more about Brand Archetypes to develop your author brand, connect with us by booking in a Book Mapping Session.

> *The concept of archetypes is aligned with neuroscience research showing that people make intuitive decisions and are driven by unconscious emotional goals.*

STEP 3
consider your brand positioning

What is your brand positioning? As with business branding, when you become an author, you need to own a position in the marketplace. Who comes to mind when you think of the best real estate author? What books have you read about finance? Who comes to mind as an author or expert in relationships?

I want you to consider yourself like that. Where do you fit into the marketplace? Which market position or authority do you want to own as an author? When it comes to brand positioning, I love to make analogies with vehicle brands—if your author brand were a car, would you be a custom-made Tesla or a family friendly Toyota? Knowing your brand positioning in the marketplace will also help you determine the pricing of your book and any related courses, services, products, or programs.

STEP 4
check your images & photographs

As a first-time author, you don't want to come across as an amateur, so invest in professional photography that will bring out your personality. Just because you're self-publishing your book doesn't mean that your images should look like you've done them yourself. Remember, you will be promoting yourself as much as your book, so make sure your images reflect your authentic self and add to your credibility. Research some authors that you like. Look at their pictures. Take note of their stance, expression, clothing, setting, and lighting. Are the images candid or staged? All these decisions help shape your author brand and personality.

STEP 5
be consistent in your brand

Consistency is king when it comes to creating a memorable author brand. Your brand personality, tone of voice, images, fonts, colours, and everything about you should be consistent across all platforms so that your audience recognises you and becomes familiar with you and your message. If your author brand ties in with your business brand, this is even more important.

Brand strategy is one of my favourite things in the world, so at Maja Creative, we help our clients create their author brands by mapping out their brand strategy, brand personality and brand positioning. We create effective brand assets that help authors raise their profile and credibility as an author.

Consistency is king when it comes to creating a memorable author brand.

chapter seventeen
inspired actions

CREATE YOUR AUTHOR BRAND

1. Establish your brand values

Brand values examples:

Abundance	Gentility	Order
Accessibility	Giving	Peace
Balance	Hardworking	People
Belonging	Health	Prosperity
Boldness	Heart	Prudence
Calmness	Intuition	Questioning
Camaraderie	Inventiveness	Realism
Care	Investing	Reason
Carefulness	Irreverence	Recognition
Daring	Joy	Support
Decisiveness	Justice	Supremacy
Delight	Kindness	Sympathy
Desire	Knowledge	Teamwork
Detailed	Leadership	Temperance
Education	Learning	Tidiness
Efficiency	Mindfulness	Timeliness
Elegance	Modesty	Uniqueness
Empathy	Neatness	Valour
Fairness	Nerve	Variety
Family	Nurturing	Warm
Ferocity	Obedience	Youthfulness
Gallantry	Openness	Zeal

Write out your brand values

2. Establish your brand personality attributes

Brand personality examples:

Accessible	Healthy	Rational
Active	Helpful	Realistic
Adaptable	Heroic	Reflective
Admirable	Innovative	Relaxed
Adventurous	Insightful	Sage
Balanced	Intelligent	Sarcastic
Big-thinking	Intense	Simple
Brilliant	Joyful	Skeptical
Capable	Kind	Scholarly
Caring	Knowledgeable	Secure
Casual	Leader	Tasteful
Decisive	Laid Back	Teacher
Dedicated	Liberal	Thorough
Deep	Luxurious	Tolerant
Determined	Masculine	Tough
Earthy	Maternal	Trusting
Earnest	Mature	Trustworthy
Easygoing	Neat	Understanding
Eccentric	Natural	Upbeat
Farsighted	Objective	Vivacious
Fatherly	Observant	Versatile
Feminine	Open	Warm
Firm	Old Fashioned	Wild
Flexible	Passionate	Wise
Generous	Patient	Wholesome
Gentle	Patriotic	Witty
Genuine	Peaceful	Worldly
Glamorous	Quiet	Youthful
Hardworking	Quirky	Zany

Write out your brand personality attributes

....
....
....
....
....
....
....

3. Consider your brand positioning. Which market position or authority do you want to own as an author?

....
....
....
....
....
....
....
....
....

4. Make sure you're using professional images and photographs.

5. Check if everything is consistent.

18

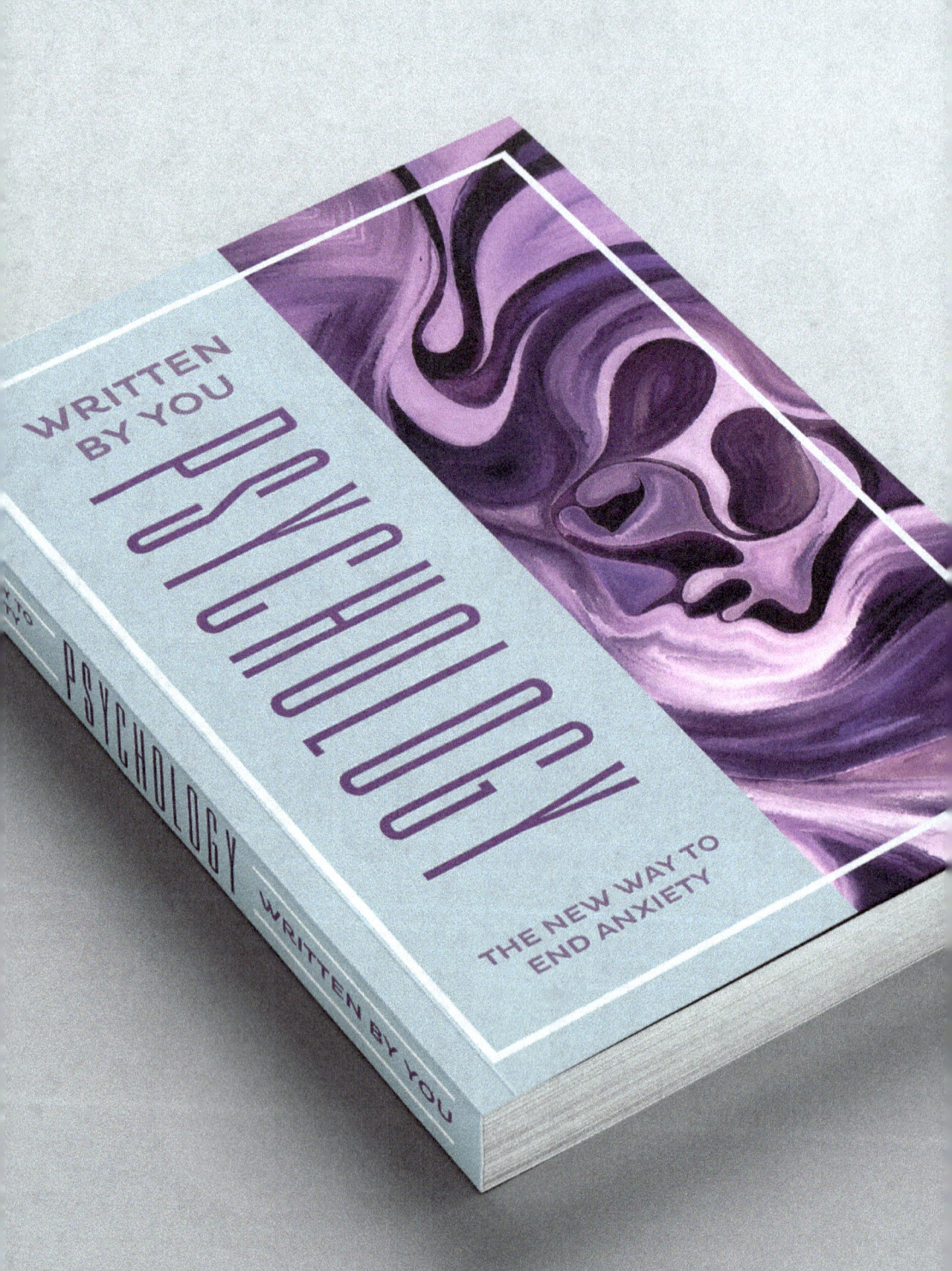

chapter eighteen

REVERSE ENGINEER
your book

Today, I have a fun exercise for you to do. I want you to use your imagination and start visualising what it will be like when you are finally a published author. How will it feel when you are holding your book in your hands? What is going to happen when you start selling your book? How many copies are you going to sell? Start to paint the picture of your life as an author.

schedule your book launch

In order to turn your dream into a reality, I want you to think about your book launch and reverse engineer the progress of your book from there. You need to give yourself a deadline. Don't leave it in the never never land of 'I'll finish it this year'. Be specific. Is it in two weeks? Is it next month? Does it coincide with a significant milestone? Give yourself a specific date and schedule it into your calendar.

When you commit to a date and publicly share it with others, you are more likely to achieve your goal. This public commitment is a crucial part in promoting your book. Once your book launch date is out in public, you'll have to deliver on your promise. This will motivate you and increase your chances of success.

STEP 1
set a date for your pre-launch

There are three dates in the calendar that you need to consider. The first date I want you to schedule is your pre-launch day. On your pre-launch, you need to have your book cover designed, your social media assets developed, and your book mocked up and your sales page set up so that you can start promoting and pre-selling your book.

STEP 2
set a date to finish your manuscript

The second date to schedule is the day that you will finish writing your manuscript. While you're promoting your book, you should be busy working on your manuscript, but you don't want this process to drag on. You'll need time to send to your editor and allow for the editing process.

Let your editor know when they should expect your manuscript. Creating this accountability gives you more incentive to stick to your deadline.

The best kind of accountability is the support of a writing community. If you haven't done so already, I encourage you to join the 20-Minute Author 20-Day Challenge and aim to finish your first draft within 20 days!

STEP 3
set a date for your book launch

The third date you need to consider is your launch day. By your launch, your edited manuscript has been professionally formatted and designed, and your book is printed and set up for downloads. On this day, you will start delivering your book, whether that means selling it online, selling it in physical shops, or giving it away if it is a freebie to promote your business.

STEP 4
plan your book launch

Decide now how you will be selling your book at your book launch. Will your book appear in brick and mortar shops? Will you be exclusively selling it online on sites like Amazon? Will you be offering it for download or purchase on your own website or landing page?

When it comes to your book launch itself, will you have an in-person launch at a bookstore? Traditional book launches give you the opportunity to give book readings and book signings in front of the media and paying customers, and they drum up early publicity and sales for your book.

> *When you commit to a date and publicly share it with others, you are more likely to achieve your goal.*

Are you considering doing a book tour? You don't have to do an elaborate multiple-city tour to launch your book; if you want a smaller tour, you can host readings and signings at different bookstores in your hometown.

Do you want to host a digital book launch? You can stream your launch on Zoom using Facebook Live or YouTube. Social media gives you the opportunity to launch your book in front of a larger audience than you could achieve in person. In fact, it is essential to stream on social media even if you choose to host an in-person launch.

All of these options are available to you, and the sky is the limit. Today, use your imagination and get excited about finally releasing your book into the world!

STEP 5:
reach out for help

When you begin the journey of self-publishing your book, you'll quickly realise that there are elements that overlap and things that need to happen simultaneously, so you will most likely reach a point where you get stuck. When this happens, please reach out for help. At Maja Creative, we reverse engineer your book launch so that you can get through the process step-by-step and publish your book this year.

If you haven't done so already, book in for your Book Mapping Session with me, and we will map out a realistic launch schedule for your book.

WRITTEN BY YOU

PSYCHOLOGY

THE NEW WAY TO END ANXIETY

chapter eighteen
inspired actions

COMMIT TO A DATE FOR BOOK SUCCESS

1. Give yourself a date when you commit to promoting your book. Decide when your book cover and book mockup will be finished and visible to the public. This is the prelaunch phase of your book when you can start preselling your book.

I will get my book cover designed and pre-launch assets completed by:

....

....

2. Give yourself a deadline for finishing your manuscript and sending it off to your editor.

I will finish my manuscript and get it to the editor on:

....

....

3. Establish your book launch date and decide when you will start delivering your book to your audience.

My book will be completed, and I will finally get to hold it in my hands on:

....

....

My official book launch will happen on:

....

....

4. Decide how and where you will sell your book. Will you have a physical or virtual book launch? Will your book be sold in stores? Will it be exclusively available online? Will it be a promotional freebie for your business?

My book launch vision is: (describe how you imagine your book launch, where will it be, who will attend, etc.)

....

....

....

....

....

....

....

....

....

5. Grab a spot in our schedule for your Book Mapping Session here: https://bit.ly/BookMappingSession

My Book Mapping Session is scheduled for

....

....

THE 20-MINUTE author
STEP-BY-STEP WORKBOOK

Your custom roadmap to write, publish and promote your book.

MAJA WOLNIK

19

STEP 1:
ask yourself why

Have a think about this idea today in the context of your book. Take a step back, and ask yourself—why do you want to become an author? Why are you writing your book? What is the purpose of your book? What is the intention that you want to achieve with your book?

- Is writing your book your end goal in itself? Will you be happy when you've completed it and ticked it off the bucket list?
- Do you have a unique story that want to share with the world?
- Do you want to use your book as a lead magnet for your business to attract dream clients and customers?
- Are you writing your book because you want to raise your profile, establish your personal brand, and increase your credibility?
- Perhaps you want to be like one of my clients who wanted to become an international speaker, and your book is a vehicle to launch you into that platform?
- Do you dream of becoming a well-known authorpreneur and make a living from writing multiple books?

STEP 2
brainstorm your reasons why

Brainstorm these ideas today and come up with the one that resonates most with you. There are no right or wrong answers here. Check in with yourself, close your eyes, listen to your heart, and think about the core purpose of why you're writing your book —the answer might surprise you!

THE 20-MINUTE AUTHOR

why do you want to become an author?

chapter nineteen

CASE STUDY
this book

Today, as we near the end of our journey together, I want to take you behind the scenes of this book. This book that you are holding and reading right now, is proof that if I can write, publish and promote a book, so can you.

When my design clients began asking me to design books, the stars magically aligned, my past experience in publishing came together, and an instant love for the medium and industry was born. As I worked with our clients and saw the struggles they faced trying to write and publish their books, I was inspired to write my own book—about writing books! What started off as a way of documenting my own journey so that I could better help my clients has now turned into this book, a 20-Day Challenge eCourse and a growing community of authors-to-be.

This journey has been nothing but fascinating, and I have covered everything in this book as I have experienced it. Today, I want to talk about the book design itself. So, let's dig in…

STEP 1
the design challenge

'They sky is the limit!' I said to Monika, our graphic designer. Her face went pale. It turns out, I am possibly the worst client ever… I wanted this to be the best, most delicious book of all time. I wanted to showcase our wild creativity and demonstrate that we can develop the most unique design possible. But how?

STEP 2
how we approached the challenge

- We sat on this for a long time…and stared at a blank page. When you are too close to a project and you are allowed to do ANYTHING…well, NOTHING happens. Good design comes about from constraints, so we decided to approach our own book project in the same way that we would approach a client's book—with a clear brief and reasonable constraints.
- The book had to appeal to our ideal reader profile of coaches, consultants, and business owners.

This journey has been nothing but fascinating, and I have covered everything in this book as I have experienced it.

- The book had to utilise the Maja Creative brand assets—colours, typeface, and imagery.
- The book had to allow for lots of text as well as double up as a workbook that could be utilised hand in hand with the 20-Minute Author 20-Day Challenge eCourse.
- The book had to provide exceptional value to our audience but also act as a portfolio showcase of our design capabilities.
- The book had to be delicious, inspiring, and fun to develop.
- The book had to have a system yet be highly creative.

STEP 3
the outcome

When you flip through the pages of this book, you will notice that we have developed a unique system to communicate and convey key information in this book. There are chapter openings to introduce each topic, as well as repeated elements that provide a consistent and cohesive look throughout the book. We have utilised our brand colours of moss green and mauve throughout, and we have created spacious workbook sections that are easy to journal and fill out.

We've had the most fun creating the images that are peppered through this book. Looking at research from our community of authors-to-be, we selected a range of books that our ideal clients are working on, and we then painstakingly custom designed each book cover as if that book was already in print. We superimposed our covers on book mock-ups that fall in line with our brand personality and overall style.

The interior pages of this book follow a Complex Book Design format with the addition of the twenty or so unique custom covers we had the absolute joy to design. If we can do this for our own book, imagine what we can achieve with yours?!

20

I AM A
WEALTHY
WOMAN
YOUR NAME HERE
I AM A
WEALTHY
WOMAN
Build your empire on your terms
YOUR NAME HERE

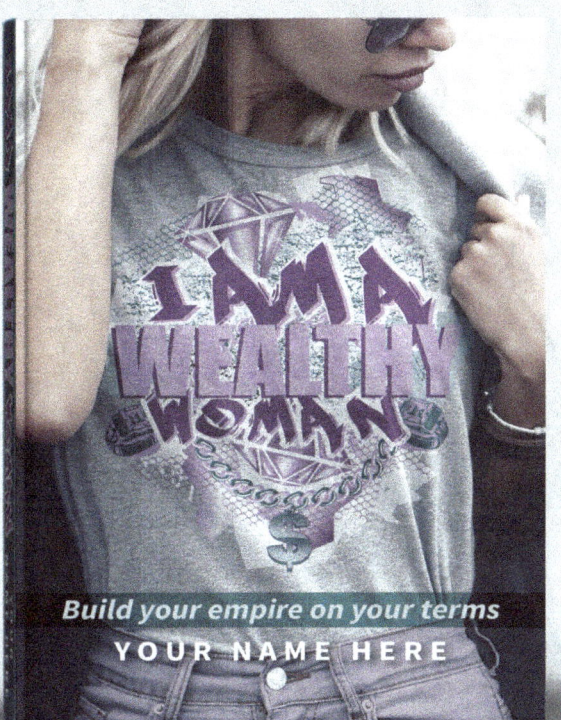

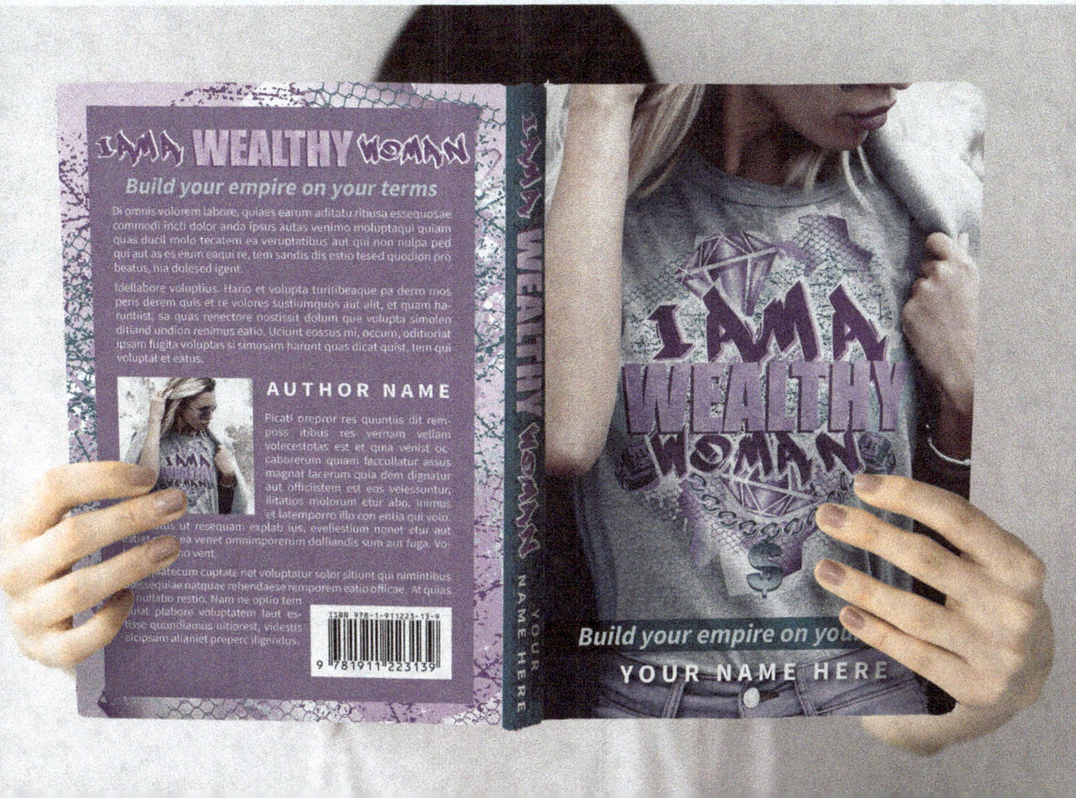
I AM A WEALTHY WOMAN
Build your empire on your terms
Di omnis volorem labore, quiaes earum aditatu rituusa essequosae commodi incti dolor anda ipsus autas venimo moluptaqui quiam quas ducil molo tecatem ea veruptatibus aut qui non nulpa ped qui aut as es eium eaqui re, tem sandis dis estio tesed quodion pro beatus, nia dolesed igent.
Idellabore voluptius. Hario et volupta turitibeaque pa derro mos peris derem quis et re volores sustiumquos aut alit, et quam haruntist, sa quas renectore nostissit dolum que volupta simolen ditiand undion renimus eatio. Uciunt eossus mi, occum, oditioriat ipsam fugita voluptas si simosam harunt quas dicat quist, tem qui voluptat et eatus.
AUTHOR NAME
Picati orepror res quuntiis dit remposs itibus res vernam veliam volecestotas est et quia venist occaborerum quiam facculiatur assus magnat lacerum quia dem dignatur aut officiistem est eos velessuntur, ilitatios molorum etur abo. Inimus et latemporro illo con entia qui volo.
ISBN 978-1-911223-13-9
9 781911 223139
I AM A WEALTHY WOMAN
YOUR NAME HERE
I AM A
WEALTHY
WOMAN
YOUR NAME HERE

chapter twenty

YOU ARE AN
author

Congratulations! You have made it to day 20 of the 20-Minute Author 20-Day Challenge! Thank you so much for sharing this journey with me. I am honoured to be your guide on this adventure.

No matter where you are right now with your book, I want you to stop and acknowledge the effort you have put in during these past weeks. I want to celebrate the person that you have become—you ARE an author! You have discovered that all you needed was a mindset shift to change your vision of yourself, coupled with consistent action. Just by reading this book and joining the 20-Minute Author 20-Day Challenge, you have taken that first courageous step.

STEP 1
celebrate your progress

Over the last 20 chapters, we have covered:

- Daily tech hacks on how to finish your book fast, using voice-to-text.
- Prompts that you need to develop your ideal reader profile.
- Strategies on how to build your audience and grow your author brand while you write.
- Mindset and how to overcome impostor syndrome.
- Best tips for professional editing of your manuscript
- Ways to make your book a bestseller by professionally designing your front and back cover.
- Interior page design that will make your book a page turner and keep your readers engaged.
- And much more...

STEP 2
declare yourself an author now

We have covered a lot of ground in this book, but I have one more tip up my sleeve! My tip for you today is to declare yourself an author today and start promoting your book NOW!

Many famous authors and second-time authors start promoting their new books the minute they decide to write them. This is a clever strategy they use to build their audience and generate hype around their book while they are still writing. Just because you are a first-time author doesn't mean that you can't do the same.

I believe that this is the best strategy to achieve success for your book long-term. You don't want to spend all this time perfecting your manuscript, creating your design, and publishing your book only to realise that you have no marketing strategy in place to get your book into the hands of your readers.

> Start promoting your book right now and share it with your audience.

You already have a network. You have clients and customers who trust you. You have friends and family that love and adore you. Start promoting your book right now and share it with your audience. Build on that audience until you have a group of raving fans who will generate word-of-mouth marketing for your book.

Here are some ideas that you can use today to begin promoting your book.

STEP 3
promote through social media

Promote your book constantly and consistently on social media and create a list of people on Facebook and Instagram who want to purchase your book when you are ready to launch. You can also create a Facebook Group for people who want to spread the word about your book when it is ready to be published. Connect with these people via FB Messenger and DM to keep them in the loop about your book. Also collect emails and especially cell phone numbers—this allows you to email and text your future readers to tell them when and where they can buy your book.

STEP 4
start preselling your book

Start preselling your book today and deliver it to your readers once it is launched. You can set up a simple shopping cart on your landing page and start collecting the money now to fund the production of your book. I love this strategy because it gives you an insight into who is interested in your book before you invest too much time, energy, and money into a promotion strategy. This kind of organic test marketing allows you to tweak your game plan before you publish.

STEP 5
launch a kickstarter campaign

Once you have some of your book assets developed, like your book cover, book sample, and social media tiles, you can create a Kickstarter campaign to promote and fund your book while you're writing it. Kickstarter also gives you a great platform for launching your book when it is published.

Your audience can help you promote and review your book.

STEP 6
reach out to the media

You can use your social media assets to generate hype and interest around your book. You can start organizing podcast interviews, and you can create a media press release kit so you can be featured in magazines and articles about your book. This is especially important if you are positioning your book to grow your personal brand as an expert in your field.

Promote your book constantly and consistently on social media.

STEP 7
write a blog about your book journey

One of the best ways to promote your book is to document your book creation journey in a blog or vlog and share it to a dedicated Instagram and Facebook account. As you write, you can share your content relating to the particular chapter that you are working on. When you share snippets of your wisdom and encourage people to follow your progress, they will engage with you on a personal level and want to buy your book as soon as it becomes available.

STEP 8
build your audience of raving fans

When you build your audience, you generate interest, desire, and anticipation for your book so by the time you are ready to publish, people can't wait to finally get your book in their hands.

Your audience can help you promote and review your book. Create a list of raving fans and send them each an advance autographed copy of your book. Ask these people to read your book and leave a 5-star review on Amazon when you have your Amazon author page set up. This is a great way to build up positive buzz about your book and create sales momentum when you launch.

chapter twenty
inspired actions

TAKE THE FINAL STEPS TO BECOMING AN AUTHOR

1. Declare yourself to be an author now.

2. Promote your book through social media.

3. Start preselling your book.

4. Launch a Kickstarter campaign.

5. Reach out to the media.

6. Document your book journey in a blog.

7. Build your audience of raving fans.

YOUR NAME HERE

Namaste
YOGA FOR THE SOUL

21

chapter twenty one

YOUR BOOK MAPPING
session

Hello, my amazing author!

You have made it to the end of this workbook, and if you've bought the eCourse, you've made it through the 20-Day Challenge! Congratulations! Well done. I'm proud of you for staying the course, and I hope that you have enjoyed the process, no matter where you are at with your book. You now have the tools to become an author and publish your book this year.

I want you to know that you have two options today. Number one is you can go ahead and implement the information from the last 20 days and make progress with your book. I genuinely believe that you can get some headway if you implement everything that you've learned and commit to working on your book for 20 minutes each day.

Now, I know that some of you will find this process really overwhelming. There are so many elements to it. So, if you don't want to do this alone, I am giving you a personal invitation today to book in for your Book Mapping Session with me.

sign up for your book mapping session

Now, I've mentioned this session a few times, so I'm just going to recap on what happens in the session. During the session, you will get an undivided hour of my time. We will go over all the elements that you need to finally become an author and publish your book. We'll do this by reverse engineering your book based on when you want to launch it, and we will develop a step-by-step, guided plan for accomplishing your book launch.

We will also develop a personalised plan for overcoming blocks so that you are able to keep on track with your writing process. Whether you feel stuck with writing, editing, or promotion, we will help you keep moving forward so that you have a published book in your hands by the end of the process.

For those of you who are fully committed to jumping on a call with me, I will unlock a special gift as a reader of this book. All you have to do is book here https://bit.ly/BookMappingSession and select an available time. These slots fill up fast! So, if you haven't booked in for yours yet, make sure to grab your spot today.

unlock your special gift

I am going to unlock a special gift for those of you who have clicked the link above and scheduled your Book Mapping Session with me.

If you take advantage of our Ultimate Author Starter Kit during our call, which includes full book cover design, we will give you a FREE book mockup** for you to use in your advertising campaign. This book mock-up includes your finished cover and sample pages, and it is an essential part of your online marketing strategy. You can take selfies or even create a professional photoshoot with this book, allowing you to promote your book while you are still writing it.

If you have any questions about the Book Mapping Session, don't be afraid to reach out, and if you are ready, make sure to book in today.

I would love to help you become an author. I am so excited that you have been here with me on this journey. My mission is to help you hold your book in your hands this year, just like the book you are holding right now.

May your book bring you abundance, and may it make an impact in the lives of those that need to hear your wisdom.

With love and light,
Maja

get the ultimate author starter kit

Start promoting your book while you add the finishing touches to your manuscript.

The Ultimate Author Starter Kit is perfect for you to get your book cover designed so you can generate interest and desire about your book NOW. Start building your audience and following as an author - even if your book is not finished!

WHAT'S INCLUDED:

- 1 x Book Mapping Session (up to 1 hour)
- 1 x Book Cover Creative Brief
- 1 x Book Cover Design (Front, Back & Spine)
- Copywriting for Book Blurb and Author Bio
- 6 x Book Mock Up images (front, back & stacked - jpegs)
- Done-for-You Social Media Pack which includes
  - Facebook & LinkedIn Banner
  - 6 x social tiles of your choice (tiles, stories, ads)
- Landing Page Mock Up (to pass onto your web developer)
- Landing Page Copywriting
- 2 x rounds of client changes
- Print ready PDF files supplied for printing
- *Bonus:* FREE Printed Book Sample**
  (one off print with placeholder text or blank pages)

*Photography, images and illustration not included.
**This offer is available to eligible applicants in Australia only unless otherwise specified.

The Ultimate author starter kit

Bonus: printed book sample!

landing page mock up

social media tiles/ad graphics

insta/fb story tiles

fb/linked in banners

mockup images

Crystal Abundance
WRITTEN BY YOU

PATIENCE & PERSEVERANCE
Life lessons from owning a shelter dog
YOUR NAME HERE

YOUR NAME HERE
POLAND
THE HEART OF EUROPE

LUXURIOUS APARTMENTS
How to make small spaces luxe
WRITTEN BY YOU

WRITTEN

YOUR NAME HERE
Namaste
YOGA FOR THE SOUL

PURPLE eats
FRUITS & VEGGIES TO FUEL YOUR SKIN
YOUR NAME

...ire on your terms
...NAME HERE

SMOOTH OPERATOR
Quick & delicious smoothie recipes
WRITTEN BY YOU

WE ARE ALL MADE OF stardust
a simple guide to astrology
WRITTEN BY YOU

more ways that we can help you

The 20-minute Author 20Day Challenge

If you love the actions in this book, use it together with the 20minute Author 20 Day Challenge online course. Visit https://majacreative.com/the-20-minute-author-challenge/ to sign up and you'll get instant access to my library of lessons and videos where I delve a little deeper into each chapter of this book. There is also a live round of the Challenge once a year and you'll get access to the 20-minute Author private Facebook Group.

Book Coaching, Writing & Editing

We'll help you develop and write your book manuscript correctly from the start and keep you on track to finish. Our team includes coaches, ghost writers and editors that will make your manuscript shine and help you co-ordinate a successful book launch.

Book Cover Design

Let's create your unique custom book cover design that will grab attention and communicate the essence of your book instantly.

We combine creative concepts with beautiful typography, images and illustrations that will appeal to your target reader. We also pay extra attention to the back cover and spine, which are just as important to establish your credibility as an author and be visible on shelf.

Your single most important marketing tool can help increase sales and compel your reader to want to read every page. We create covers for paper back and hardcover printed books as well as digital and audio books.

Book Interior Page Design

Let's create a beautiful reading experience for your audience with professionally designed book pages, typesetting and formatting.

No book is the same, that's why we specialise in high quality custom-designed book interiors where each page can be uniquely designed and typeset based on your needs to create a masterpiece.

Book Promotion & Author Branding

We can develop all the marketing tools you need to promote your book. From press kits, bookmarks, social media assets and campaigns to promotional postcards, pull up banners and keynote presentations for your book launch. We also specialise in author branding which can include professional photography, logo design and marketing collateral to establish your credibility as an author.

Self-publishing Assistance

If you're feeling confused and overwhelmed by the self-publishing process, we'll help you navigate this new terrain with our easy step-by-step process. We'll help you co-ordinate all aspects and take care of the nitty gritty details like ISBN codes, barcodes, printing specifications and file uploads so you can concentrate on your manuscript only.

You can find out about all our services and offers by visiting www.majacreative.com

Thank you!

thank you note

This book could not have come together without the help and support of so many amazing people who have cheered me on throughout this journey.

Firstly, to my beautiful clients, thank-you for continuing to inspire me with your incredible books that I've had the absolute honour and pleasure to help you birth into the world. Sharing your challenges inspired me to create this book.

Thank-you to my wonderful team! Monika, you have taken this mega book project on as if it was your own, and made my creative vision come to life better than what I could have imagined it to be. Thank-you for your tenacity, creativity and ability to manoeuvre through the most tedious aspects with grace. Belinda, thank-you for single handedly taking care of everything else digital to accompany this book with your incredible enthusiasm and encouragement. Lena, thank-you for all that you do.

Paula, thank-you for all that you are and all that you do. You support is pure magic and I wouldn't be half the woman that I have become, let alone publish this book, without your guidance and truth.

Bruce, thank-you for your unwavering support, encouragement and accountability. I'm so grateful to have you in my corner.

Sabina, thank-you for helping me clear all the blocks and transforming my mind to believe. I am forever so grateful for the power of your work.

Caitlin, thank-you so much for all your guidance, knowledge and sharp editing. You took my mess of transcriptions and turned it into a brilliant manuscript for my book. I am so grateful we met randomly online and have developed such an incredible collaboration.

To my amazing friends and girlfriends, you know who you are, thank-you for cheering me on, always.

To Flick (Twinno), thank-you for being a true friend, for all our strategising and laughs and manifesting support. I'm so grateful for you soul sister.

To my beautiful family, Gosia, Janusz, Kasia, Radek, Ela and Sebastian and my extended family, thank-you for always being there for me, for all your love and understanding and supporting yet another one of my creative endeavours with the same enthusiasm as the very first one. Love you.

To my fur babies, Zuzia and Leila, thank-you for being the best company and the best distractions when writing and creating this book.

To my amazing authors-to-be, thank you for giving me purpose, I'm here to serve you and this book is proof that if I can do this, you can do this too.

Thank-you to all who bought this book even before it was born, thank-you for your patience!

And to the universe, thank-you for your magic and for always having my back. Thank you for the trip to the cabin, where I dreamt a beautiful dream of a life filled with books and babies, and my vision of my destiny rolled out in front of me.

With love and light,
Maja xx

stay connected

Come and say hi to me on social media and let me know what kind of book you're working on – I'd love to hear from you!

Instagram @maja.wolnik or @maja.creative
Facebook @majawolnik or @majacreative
LinkedIn @majawolnik

about the author

Maja Wolnik is a passionate creative director, brand strategist, and author. Her design agency, Maja Creative, helps coaches, consultants, entrepreneurs, business owners, and other experts become published authors. By writing their books, her clients are able to share their wisdom, leverage their expertise, and build a passive income stream.

Maja is committed to helping heart-centredand purpose-driven business owners build meaningful, memorable, and successful brands that positively impact the community and the world.

Prior to launching Maja Creative, Maja clocked over 20,000 expert hours honing her skills in the fields of graphic design, branding, marketing, and brand strategy, working in-house, in-studio, and freelance. She has worked in a broad range of industries, including government, manufacturing, travel, advertising, retail, and publishing.

Her breadth of experience over the last decade—including working and living across three different continents in Poland, Canada, and Australia—has given her a unique worldly view of people and business. She received her Bachelor of Arts in Creative Advertising from RMIT University. She has studied fine art at Melbourne University, Direct Marketing at ADMA, and Illustration at Emily Carr University.

Maja's magic skill is to listen with empathy and translate her clients' visions into reality. She focuses on the latest neuroscience research to connect with people's hearts and minds, helping her clients create brands and books that inspire, empower, and delight.

www.ingramcontent.com/pod-product-compliance
Lightning Source LLC
Chambersburg PA
CBHW070621010526
44108CB00052B/1974